A LIFE DISCOVE[RED]

Introduction

Father Hudson was a Catholic priest who foun[d] orphaned children and brought in waifs and strays from inner-city Birmingham in the early years of the 20th century. From the early years of the preceding century a number of laws had been passed controlling the working conditions of children, but that century saw many children living on the streets. A philanthropist of his time, Father Hudson focused strongly on the social issues of the day, particularly health, medical treatment and education. He also laid emphasis on the moral and spiritual welfare of those who would come into the care of the Catholic diocese. One criterion for accepting a child was that its Catholic faith was in danger, not just that it was in physical want or danger.

The home that I lived in was built in the Warwickshire countryside in 1905. The whole complex was huge, occupying several acres of land. Father Hudson knew that when an orphan left a Home he would have to fend for himself, and education would be his best hope, and to this end he set up not only an orphanage with a chapel, but a hospital, a nursery, a school, and a working boys' hostel, where boys could learn a proper trade.

His kindly face looked down from a photograph in the Chapel cloisters. The floor of the Chapel cloister was marble, highly polished six days a week, and forbidden territory except to meet a visitor. My job when I was five was to dust both Church and Chapel, so I saw Father Hudson's picture every day. But did his spirit live on in the institution he had founded?

On the whole, the whole place ran like clockwork; rather like an army barracks, starting with prayers as a nun opened the dormitory, and closing with a blessing as you lay down to sleep. The whole identity of the institution was specifically Catholic in doctrine and practice, and these beliefs infused the whole establishment on a daily basis. It was compulsory to attend Mass every Sunday and on the eight Holy Days of Obligation such as St Peter and Paul's day, to say the Rosary every day with one of the nuns, to go to confession once a month.

Everybody has walked past a church. What is going on inside? Everybody knows the power of bells, the power of stained glass, the power of high *vaulted roofs, the power of communal singing. Everybody has felt the mystery of sacred places, from Stonehenge to Mecca.*

This is my story; the story of a boy brought up in Father Hudson's Home for boys, from November 1965 at the age of three years and ten months, until he was sixteen.

Chapter One

There I was, in the nursery, St Teresa's. It smelled cacky. But outside in the yard there were toys. In the dormitory, by the big window, was a wardrobe full of teddy bears which we could take to bed at night. Life was peaceful. One of the nurses took a liking to me. And there I sat, in her room, in the early hours of the morning, playing with her hair rollers and hiding them in my pocket. Somewhere, bells were ringing. It was time for church, said the nurse. So we walked out of the nursery, through the grounds of Father Hudson's, to the church.

I remember Canon Flint, face to the altar and its religious icons, groaning gobbledygook. In those days, the Mass was celebrated in Latin and Greek. *'Kyrie eleison, Christe eleison'* he chanted, and the people echoed his mysterious words. I was four, and lived in the nursery of the Home. Incense wafted through the air, while I played with the hair rollers and clips which I had hidden in my pockets.

Later, at five, in 1967, I moved from the nursery to St Edward's Home itself. The nun Sister Mary Xavier was given the task of looking after me and my friend Paul Wright. She wore a white starched habit from neck to ankles, large black lace-up boots, a big white starched veil which hid all her hair and showed only her face, and a large silver and black crucifix round her neck. On Sundays the nuns' habits and veils were black. She took us to our new home; we walked through the grounds into the chapel cloister to meet her. Later I learned that she was called Cruncher because of the way she continuously ground her false teeth. Her glasses had very thick lenses, and she played the organ in chapel and in church.

The dormitories were huge. The home was divided into houses; mine was Our Lady's, the smallest house; we were twenty-four boys. We slept in the high-ceilinged dormitory with partitions between our iron bedsteads, while a tall statue of Our Lady, the Virgin Mary, the mother of Jesus, watched us. She was standing on the moon, and treading on a snake, with her hands held together in prayer. There was a strong smell of Johnson's Wax. At night we were locked in. We made our own beds every morning. If a boy wet his bed, he would do his best to swap his sheets with yours, so that he didn't have to wash them. Wet sheets had to be carried down to the laundry and dumped into the huge sinks. Then they had to be bashed in soapy water with a brass dolly. The next port of call was the bathroom, where we bathed using pungent carbolic soap. We cleaned our teeth with pink or blue tooth powder which came in a round tin and tasted chalky. I missed the small scale happy atmosphere of the nursery; St Edward's was terrifying from the outset. From then on I lived in a constant state of fear until I reached adolescence.

From the window of my new frightening dormitory we could see Father Hudson's grave, and as I walked past it I was told the inscription said 'Suffer little children to come unto me'.

The dormitory windows could only be opened by about nine inches, to prevent boys from 'bunking it'. But some succeeded, at least for a while. A family of 'escaping' travellers was featured on the ATV Midland News, and we watched avidly.

The regime was very strict, and bullying was rife. The older boys used the younger ones as if they were slaves. We regularly had to hand over our breakfasts; or own up to things we hadn't done and take the punishments the nuns meted out. Sometimes the punishment was to miss your breakfast anyway. I had to act as slave to a particular boy (let's call him Leroy for convenience), who used to set me impossible tasks as a joke. 'Go and fetch the toilet' he ordered one day. I wondered what this meant, but I went upstairs, stood on the toilet seat, and reached up to collect the potty from the high shelf above it. I thought this was quite clever. Leroy didn't think so and beat me up.

The sweet shop was opened on a Saturday; we had a little pocket money to spend every week, and some was saved for an annual holiday at Penmaenmawr; one of the highlights of the year. When we had our six weeks' summer school holidays each of the four houses and two houses of the cottage homes would take it in turn to have a week's holiday in Penmaenmawr, by the seaside in North Wales. The house had been bought by Canon Flint, as Sister Xavier would remind us, and we would have to be on our best behaviour because she called the people that lived there 'select people'. Perhaps this was an Irish expression meaning respectable? It was right next door to the Catholic Church, which was run by the Franciscan Friars, the Capuchins.

In the playroom at Our Lady's there were big wooden glazed picture frames holding pictures of the 'old boys', as they were always known to us, in tents in fields. The nickname for the holiday was always 'camp', because of this history of camping holidays. It was one of the highlights of the year and in true military style each boy would have a brown suitcase with a tag on its handle with your name; 'Karl Bicknell'. It was put on top of the long wooden chest of drawers, where we kept our toys, comics and letters and other bits and pieces. The nun, Sister Xavier, a bit of a perfectionist, would then read out; 'three khaki shorts, three T-shirts, one pair of beach sandals, one Sunday best pair of trousers...'; she read out a whole list of things to put into the suitcase, and then in the evening when the job was complete it was time to say the rosary to pray for good weather.

If you misbehaved you got no pocket money at all that week. I was lucky; the nurse who had known me in the nursery left to get married (I was allowed to go to the wedding) and her mother used to send me a parcel every week, containing the Beano, the Dandy and some sweets. Older boys used to say 'Can I read your comic and I'll be your best friend?' Of course it never lasted. I couldn't read the comics myself, but I liked looking at the pictures. So there were occasional happy escapes from the strictly regimented passage of our time.

This regime started every morning when Sister Xavier or Sister Francis came into the dormitory to recite early morning prayers. We could always tell which one was on her way by the sound of the keys jangling at her belt. We changed into our 'day clothes'; khaki shorts, T-shirt and pullover. Then it was down to breakfast. There were prayers before breakfast and after breakfast; next we cleared the plates up, before each child had to embark on a different cleaning job. The hall had to be cleaned; the laundry, the bathrooms, the convent, chapel, passages, dormitories. This kind of strict regime had been under dispute between Father Hudson and the nuns for many years. Ultimately his way of dealing with the conflict was to let the nuns have as much power as possible.

One day I decided I wasn't going to do my regular task of cleaning the chapel. Sister Francis, who was Sister Xavier's deputy, and very much revered, was in charge of this work, and she came to find me in the dormitory. "Why aren't you down in the chapel?" she screamed. "Because I don't want to work in the chapel any more." At that point she went red in the face, grabbed my hair, and pulled me around until tufts of it came out. Then she frog-marched me from the dormitory all the way down to the chapel. That behaviour I would never repeat; Sister Francis was small but ferocious and we all feared the month when she deputized while Sister Xavier went on holiday or retreat.

Many crimes resulted in beatings. I was beaten for talking at night, and for getting up too early on a Saturday. We were beaten with the 'quack'; a double leather strap about two foot long. On your hand it stung; on your back the marks would last for hours.

When our domestic duties were done, it was upstairs again to change into your school uniform, and off to school. At first, in Mrs Martin's class, things went well for me. We painted, did sums, and tried to learn our letters. At the end of the school day came my favourite lesson of all; story time. We all sat on the floor while Mrs Martin read to us. I don't remember what she read; I just remember the contrast of this peaceful episode with the rest of the day in the home. School dinners were better than the food in the home, but not by much.

After my time with Mrs Martin I went to St Edward's School. This had been opened in October 1914 as a school for Father Hudson's boys. In 1925 it had been taken over by the local board of education and took in children from the local parish as well as those from the Home. So there was a division between the 'Umboys' (from the home) and the Dayboys. The Junior School of St Edward's lay within the grounds, so we walked out of the door and into school.

Time to change into our day clothes again; tea at half past four in the refectory. About two dozen of us sat at four tables. In would come a huge enamel pot of tea, milk and sugar already included, to be poured into our hard green plastic cups. Food was dished out from a huge pan onto Pyrex plates; sometimes it was sausages, floating like boats on grease, while the slightly scorched beans lay beneath them to be dredged up by the ladle. I remember a loveable, extroverted little boy called Andy. He was brave; he was cheerful; he had the nerve to tease the bull in the field beside the Home. One day during tea he suddenly stabbed his Pyrex plate with his fork. The Pyrex shattered across the table, and he burst into tears. Sister Francis flew down the room and slapped him a tremendous blow. I vividly remember my feelings of total horror and helplessness. I hated her for this; I can't have been alone.

After tea we washed up again, before kneeling together to recite the rosary. One Our Father, ten Hail Mary's, one Glory Be, times five. That is called a decade of the rosary, and five of them seemed to last for ever.
(The Rosary is a way of meditating on the life of Jesus by associating incidents in that life with a series of repetitive prayers, and keeping your place in that series with a string of beads.)

Six evenings a week I and a few others had to clean the church; I dusted the long pews. Eventually I was promoted to cleaning the sanctuary. I had to scrub the marble floor once a week, and clean all the wax off the big brass candlesticks on the altar, and from the inside of the tall candle snuffer. This called for a good deal of scraping with a knife, and much polishing with Brasso and steel wool. The steel wool left a pattern of fine lines engraved in the brass.

This work meant that we arrived back in the Home at 6.00; just in time for the ATV news, having missed all the cartoons. The TV had slatted doors, and a padlock which could be locked by Sister Xavier to ensure that we couldn't change channels. On one occasion she ran across from the convent at full speed, because she had noticed in the TV guide that 'Carry on Camping' was on, and we definitely couldn't be allowed to watch that.

In the day room, with its Victorian-style florid patterned wallpaper, there was a snooker table, and several other tables at which we could play snakes and ladders, chess, draughts and so on in the winter months. Sister Francis ruled here, when Sister Xavier left for supper, and arbitrated disputes about the rules. In fine weather we played in the grounds; but the boundary of the grounds was the boundary of our world. It was a closed universe; almost our only glimpse of the outside world came from the TV. Once we saw General Booth's Salvation Army granddaughter being interviewed by Michael Parkinson. "It's a pity she hasn't the Faith," said Sister Xavier sadly in her strong Irish brogue.

Almost all the nuns were Irish. We even learned Irish dancing; "one two tree four five six seven, one two tree, one two tree". On St Patrick's Day all of us, Asian children, Afro-Caribbeans, white children and all, wore shamrocks together. There were fifteen verses to 'O glorious St Patrick, dear saint of our isle', which had to be sung every year. His non-ecological treatment of snakes would not pass muster today.

After watching TV, it was time for supper, which consisted of gruel. Big enamel jugs held this watered-down mixture of milk and oatmeal porridge, and we drank it from our green plastic mugs every evening.

Presently school became more difficult. I had such problems in learning to read and write. I tried to be good, but trying to learn was so hard that I grew furious with frustration. Everybody else in the class could do this magic trick with text, and I couldn't. The whole experience was very agitating. I tried to read one word at a time, but I couldn't get them to string together to make a story. How could everybody else do it when I couldn't? I couldn't write, either, that was even worse. It was totally alienating; I must have something the matter with me; maybe this is why I'd been sent to the Home? My first recollection of this was in Mrs Corrigan's class. Children in the class would get lollipops and pear-drops for good behaviour and good work. I hardly ever did. So I was soon disruptive and 'difficult'. I was constantly in trouble; I became a bully, stealing lunchboxes, leading a gang and thumping other kids. It seemed that I was always in Sister Catherine's office getting caned. And if I'd been swearing, I'd be punished when I got back to the home, too; Sister Francis would put mustard on my tongue and make me stand in the corner.

I started lessons to prepare for my first Holy Communion. We were each given a simple prayer book, which I couldn't read, and Sister Catherine would teach us the importance of going to mass. She taught us the form of the service, what it was all about, and that when the priest said the special words, the bread and wine would be transformed into Jesus.

We were all taught that God was once born into the world as a man (at Christmas), lived, taught, died on a cross (on Good Friday) and rose from the dead (on Easter Sunday). For Catholics, internal beliefs about God are celebrated in external rituals and representations. The Mass is a ritual celebration of the death of Jesus, a bit like a play, and it was celebrated every day in the chapel that I cleaned. A Holy Day of Obligation is a feast to celebrate some particular occasion in the life of Jesus. All Catholics at that time were expected to make regular confession of their misdeeds to a priest, who would absolve them from their guilt if their remorse seemed genuine.

Before making their first Holy Communion, every child has to make their first Confession. I was very apprehensive about mine. On the other hand, I was half-expecting that I might be transformed by this magical experience. Maybe I would become good, or things would be better?

Chapter Two

It was 1971. I was 9. One day, Sister Xavier came into the dormitory. "I've been looking everywhere for you, I've sent the boys looking for your father; here, quickly, get ready, you don't want to keep the man waiting, he wants to take you out."

I put on my yellow pullover (which she called my Val Doonican) and my green slacks, thinking to myself, '*I hope he's rich.*' I came running down the cloister and there he was...

'*Oh it's **you**; I remember **you**,*' I thought. I stood there for what seemed a long time, looking at him. '*Maybe she's better now,*' I thought, '*maybe I can get out of here now*'. I looked around to see if my mother was there; but she wasn't. We stood there for a moment. He was a miner, a face-worker; a big, well-built, black-haired, brown-eyed man, standing with Sister Xavier and Mother Teresa - a plump nun, who spoke as though always out of breath. Then he took me out in a car; a Ford Anglia, he didn't drive it himself. One of his friends drove.

I wondered if I was going home?

The man was my father, John Bicknell. He was born in 1940, a war baby, and almost completely illiterate according to my mother. Maybe he was dyslexic like myself?

I was born to him and his wife Georgina Kathleen Francesca née Pasticcio, on 13.01.1962. So what was I doing in the care of the nuns?

On 16.11.1965, when I was nearly four, my mother took the advice of her doctor, and placed me in the care of Father Hudson's Society. I had been there for five years when my father came to take me out.

What is Father Hudson's Society? What was it like then and why? Why did my mother make her decision? This narrative is an attempt to explore these questions and to set childhood memories in an adult framework of understanding. In adulthood I have been identified as dyslexic; I have been through much therapeutic work to try to resolve these issues about the past; I have gained a diploma in education; I have travelled around Europe; I have met others who have undergone similar experiences. I hope that this adult background can enable me to use my fractured childhood to help others understand the significance and the importance of childhood for those in care.

My father came each week to take me out. I greatly feared the possibility of losing him; I had something that the other boys did not have. He was a defence against the bullies; "I'll set my Dad on you!"

Saturday came again and I got myself dressed. Again he came to meet me in the chapel cloister. There happened to be a jumble sale in the St John's Hall over the road so we went over with a crowd of other boys. We were joking about how the same women were always at the front of the queue for every jumble sale, always looking for a bargain. My father moved off to explore the stalls, and I lost sight of him for a moment. The room was packed, so I went up the stairs of the hall to look for him, and stood in the gallery.

I could see him on the tombola stall, so I went downstairs to watch him. He won a prize. The prize was a game; it had a mirror and some round disks with patterns on them that you could put inside the drum; when you spun it around they would reflect off the mirror, rather like a kaleidoscope. He gave it to me.

At four o'clock the jumble sale ended and we both walked back to the Home and into the ante-refectory, where we did the washing up. There he stood talking to Sister Xavier. I overheard him saying "She loved the others but she didn't love that one. His mother is highly strung and very musical; she played both piano and accordion. I would have him down in Cardiff tomorrow but the wife would divorce me."

Was this true? Georgina came of Italian stock, born in Cardiff of an Italian immigrant businessman. I have inherited her gift for music and play the penny whistle by ear. Why did she not love 'that one'? Was she suffering from post-natal depression? How much was known about this condition then?

"Will you come up for his first Holy Communion?" asked Sister Xavier. I sat there hoping that he would say yes.
"No I can't, I have to go back to Cardiff."

"Would you see the Canon before you go?"
"Yes."
So we went to see Canon Flint in the main office. I hoped I could go home. There he stood, an elderly man, not very tall, in his black suit and white dog-collar, smoking his pipe, wearing his round-rimmed glasses. I'd never been in this 'central office' before. There was an unpleasant smell of smoke. On his big desk stood a large old-fashioned black telephone. The telephone cable ran through the air, all the way up to the ceiling, not attached to the wall.

Another smaller desk stood at the side with a typewriter on it. Maybe I'll go home if I'm good, I thought, sitting on the chair looking out of the window, hoping the Canon would not talk to my father about me misbehaving in school. Inside I was just hoping to get out of this place. If I offer the Canon some sweets it will show him that I'm good. I offered him some liquorice allsorts that my dad had given me.
"No thank you," said the Canon, "would you go back to Sister Xavier, I need to talk to your father."

Canon Flint had worked in Father Hudson's since 1944. He had in fact been instrumental in bringing me from Bradford to St Teresa's nursery four years earlier.

So I said goodbye to him and went back to the Home. The next week it was my first Holy Communion. I still hoped that my father would come, but inside I knew that he would not. But there was still a possibility that he *might*, I spent the week hoping and praying that he would.

The big day came. The girls from St Joan's all wore bridal dresses and veils; the boys wore Sunday school uniform of maroon blazer and black trousers, with a blue shirt and a blue and maroon tie. Added to this was a sash with medal. I walked down the aisle of the church, holding the prayer book which I still couldn't read. I looked round the benches of the church, but my father wasn't there. We had a party afterwards up at the church hall. Then we all went for a walk. It should have been a really special day, but for me it was a huge disappointment. I felt so miserable that I went up to the dormitory and spent the rest of the afternoon there.

In the evening I sat crying on the stairs and Sister Xavier came up:

"Why are you crying?"
"When I get older I'm going to see my Dad but I'm not going to see my Mum".
She laughed. She had no idea how important this day had been for me, or why I might be so distraught.
"You're always laughing at me", I said.
"Come on now, go to bed."

Life continued, but my father ceased to visit. After six weekends he didn't come any more.

'*She loved the others but she couldn't love that one*'. I already had a memory of a sister, and that memory was triggered suddenly. I used to call her Flancine (for Francine). At least now I knew she really existed.

As I grew I absorbed more and more about the teachings of the church; I learned to recite the entire mass by heart; I internalized the teachings and they gradually became integrated as part of my identity. This was an institutionalized Christian one. Every practice, every picture, every prayer every day, reflected this. No other world view was allowed to present itself; as I've said even the TV was under lock and key. The home echoed a monastic life-style, and the rule that the nuns lived by permeated every aspect of our lives. We didn't go shopping; the VG van came to deliver our food. We never went outside the grounds. The cinema came to us; we watched carefully-chosen films in the theatre. Even the doctor came to us; we never went to an outside surgery.

The emotional needs of the children in the home were supposedly met by religious practices and 'devotions'. We did not know that we were deprived; children accept their lives as normal; what you don't know, you don't know. The priests and nuns who ran Father Hudson's had in some sense chosen to live this life for themselves, but in turn they imposed it on the children in their care. This was standard practice at the time in similar Catholic institutions all over Britain.

School at St Edwards was going from bad to worse. I was constantly in trouble with Sister Catherine, and presently things got so bad that I was referred to a child psychiatrist to find out what the underlying problem was.

I was bullying other children by now, and thieving. One day things reached a crisis. I had cut up another boy's painting with a pair of scissors. The teacher came across and slapped me across the legs, so I lunged at her with the scissors and stabbed her in the hand. The following day Sister Catherine came into the classroom and told me to go back to the Home. I later found out that I had been expelled.

I was referred to an assessment centre, where I lived for several weeks while the staff observed me. My main fear was that I would be moved again; I'd been rejected once, was it going to happen again? Did nobody realize what it might be like to learn that I had a family; I had a father, and I had learned from him that I had a mother, sister, brothers, all living at home – and they didn't want me? Why had I never had a Christmas card from them, a birthday card, or even a letter? Did nobody realize quite how lonely and isolated I felt?

The assessment centre was very like a hospital. There was a matron, nurses, and a school, all in the same grounds. I remember playing 'snap' in one of my lessons. All in all, it was a perfectly nice set-up, but all the time I wondered *'what is so wrong with me that I'm here?'* The only familiar thing was the parcel of comics from Mrs Batty, which continued to arrive. I still couldn't read them properly, but they meant I still had some connection with the Home.

During my stay I sent a letter, which I remember copying from my teacher, to Canon Coyne, written in red crayon, trying to maintain contact and show that I wanted to remain friends. This letter survives.

I never found out what the assessors said about me. In the end Canon Coyne came to collect me and took me back to Father Hudson's. I was taught for a while by the Mother Superior, on my own. She went on and on trying to teach me to read, without success.

At last in 1971 I was sent to Forest Oak Special School in Chelmsley Wood. At the time, schools like this for the Educationally Sub-Normal were established for those with IQs below 70. Probably many dyslexic children like myself were wrongly placed in such schools. Dyslexia was not properly recognized in this country at the time (the British Dyslexia Association was not founded until 1984); certainly at St Edwards no one understood that I needed any special kind of teaching in order to learn to read.

On my first day I remember I was deeply embarrassed. Sister Xavier took me across the road to wait for the bus, and I felt frightened, and awkwardly different from those I had grown up with.

But at Forest Oak the educational system was much more relaxed than at St Edwards, and an enlightened teacher called John Moore realized something about my difficulty. He took us all right back to the beginning of the reading process and taught us the phonetics of English. We had to learn all the combinations of letters which are called 'blends' such as 'bl, cl, gl' etc. He taught me that 'Y' is sometimes a vowel. Gradually things became clearer. Eventually I found I could read the 'Famous Five' books (in the toilet late at night when I couldn't sleep). Writing remained a problem, in fact I was only liberated in adult life by the advent of the word processor; that marked the beginning of my true education.

Meanwhile the whole approach to our schooling was different at Forest Oak. We had a different teacher and a different classroom for every subject, just as most children encounter at secondary school nowadays. I liked this new system; I settled down and began to enjoy myself.

As I progressed, and moved up into the senior school at Forest Oak, my reports improved dramatically. I was picked for the school play; I played the recorder at assembly. So school began to go well. But meanwhile the loss of my father, and the total lack of any contact with my family - the lack of Christmas cards, the lack of birthday cards, the lack of letters – periodically left me grieving and melancholy.

Chapter Three

I didn't know it, but radical changes were taking place in the '70s. Fewer children were coming into children's homes because of changes in the law on abortion and changes in social attitudes to unmarried mothers and illegitimacy, and more and more the emphasis in the country at large was on returning children to their families or on placing them in other families for foster care or adoption. Meanwhile the Second Vatican Council of 1972 brought about upheaval in the Catholic Church. The mass was no longer to be said in Latin, but in the local native tongue. Monks and nuns were suddenly encouraged to wear ordinary clothes instead of all-enveloping habits, and by law those who cared for children had to be trained and qualified. At Father Hudson's these changes were far-reaching and seemed cataclysmic. The nuns were suddenly wearing short skirts and ordinary dresses and their veils were shorter and less intimidating. Sister Francis who had beaten me so hard went on a social work course where she was taught to talk to her charges, and smile. It was very confusing, but a great improvement. The ceilings of the dormitories were lowered; we acquired our own wardrobes, and carpet was laid on the floor.

But although the nuns' habits had changed, their attitude to the priesthood didn't. I remember the priest's breakfast, brought every morning by one of the nuns, and carried past me as I went to clean the chapel. A silver cover over the bacon and eggs; toast in a rack, cut neatly into triangles with crusts removed; a large pot of fresh coffee. Priests were put on pedestals and doted on. This was partly because the Catholic church teaches that the priest has been called by God and has the power to celebrate the sacraments, uphold Catholic doctrine and absolve sins, and partly because they were the only males in that enclosed society

I was talking to Sister Xavier upstairs as we did from time to time. "Your father, he was a lovely man. You shouldn't be here, you should be at home but your mother didn't want you there. Canon Flint brought you here."

Canon Flint knew my mother and father in Bradford and had collected me from there to place me in the children's home in 1965.

"You're not daft," Sister Xavier went on. "You shouldn't have been in that Special School. It's just that Sister Catherine couldn't cope with you. All the other nuns wanted to have you put somewhere else. Father Tucker's your social worker now."

Somehow I knew that she loved me. She defended me against all nuns. I knew what a social worker was; mine was called Teresa Fitzsimons. Social workers used to come once in a blue moon to ask us 'how we were?' That was the limit of their responsibility as far as I knew. So how could Father Tucker suddenly be my social worker?

Father Tucker had arrived at the home in 1975, the first qualified social worker on the staff. As my social worker, he was in fact responsible for my mental, social, and physical health, and as this was a Catholic institution, he was responsible for my spiritual well-being as well. He had a duty of care. But above all, he was responsible for the overall spiritual well-being of Father Hudson's as a community. I was still pondering on and off about my father's visits and what he had meant when he said 'she loved the others but she didn't love that one'. This poisonous seed had grown into a poisonous plant in my mind.

By this time I was thirteen. One day coming down the cloister to do my job in the chapel I was curious to know what my new social worker was like, so I knocked on the door of the priest's dining room. I wanted to check him out and find out what he looked like and what sort of personality he was.

"Hello," came Father Tucker's soft Irish voice from inside the room. I walked into the dining room thinking of something to say. He sat at the end of a huge table. To his right hung an enormous picture of a man in a cassock and gown with a red sash and a red hat; Cardinal Griffin. Father Tucker himself was a young man; ordained a year early, he initially worked at Perry Bar as a curate, while attending Aston University to train in social work. Brown-haired, of medium build, a handsome looking man, he inspired trust.

"Isn't it amazing how the Old Testament foretells the New?" I said (this seemed like a suitable opening gambit). As I talked I could hear him saying to himself: "If you understand the child you understand the parent."

What did he mean? *He knows something about me*, I thought, *but I don't know what*. I felt a little frightened of him. It was an unnerving instinctive gut fear.

"Yes," he said.

Father Tucker must have been fully aware of my circumstances. He had access to all my records; in those days they were legally available to him but not to me. Later I became aware of the fact that he seemed to deal with the more 'difficult cases'. This remark was in direct contradiction of his apparently non-judgmental attitude. How much did he 'understand the parent'? How much could he possibly have known about post-natal illness? How many of his interviews with me were simply the exercise of carefully-honed technique and how many were authentic encounters? How much had he read about Neuro-Linguistic Programming?

He presented himself as non-judgmental, and as being somehow outside the rigid system of Father Hudson's. He was very different from Canon Coyne, who was very austere and unapproachable. I grew to like and admire Father Tucker. He was a very intellectual man; one boy I knew described his homilies as 33" records with only one hit, but he was easy to talk to. I would come home from school and sometimes knock on his window and talk to him, and I used to clean his car for him. So as the year went past I saw him every day, either in chapel or to chat to. Gradually I grew to trust him.

Finally one day I plucked up the courage to ask about my mother. "I will look into it for you."

After some weeks thinking about my question I wondered *'Why is it taking so long for him to find out?'* I plucked up the courage to remind him. He was working late one night when I went to his office and knocked on the window as usual. I asked about my mother again and he told me to come around to the back door, and gave me the key. I opened the door and went in and we met in the main office. He told me to go upstairs and, as I had never been upstairs before, I felt a little uncomfortable. Clearly this interview was going to be important and different in some way. He came up the stairs behind me, carrying a file full of papers, and directed me to a small room where there were two chairs, one facing the window and the other facing into the room.

He offered me the chair facing into the room. We sat down facing each other.

This seemed a new, closed environment, quite different from our former open encounters. He opened the records on his lap, looked up and said: "You came into care at eighteen months old……. you have three step-brothers and a step-sister..." He went on to say their names …… Francine, Shaun, Stefan, Paul. I was shocked. This could only mean that I was illegitimate. It must mean that my mother had had an affair with somebody else, and I was his child, not the child of John Bicknell. "….your father came but you did not recognise him……." These announcements were carefully paced, with long pauses between each one.

I felt quite confused and disoriented. I *had* recognized my father. I knew all about my father coming and taking me out. In retrospect, I realise he was probably implying that my biological father had called, and I had not recognized *him*.

There was a pause. But the pause was not long enough this time for me to interrupt; he moved; the records on his knee slipped and looked as though they were going to fall and he grabbed them, distracting me. Suddenly his focus shifted. *This kind of moving an interview about, shifting, disconcerting, making sudden interruptions, is all typical of the therapeutic techniques of neuro-linguistic programming; my first unwitting experience of being manipulated by a 'therapist'.*

"Did you know that you were going to be adopted at one time?"
I said nothing; I had a vague memory of going out with a strange couple in a car, when I was very little, and still in the nursery, but adoption had never been discussed.

"Your mother divorced in 1974." I had the feeling that this divorce must have been entirely my fault and looked down. Something felt wrong. I could see letters in the file.
"Can I look at my mother's writing?" I asked.
"No, these letters belong to your mother, but here is a letter saying she has sent on your milk tokens." I felt confused, and bereft. Here he seemed to be offering me connection with my family, with my history, and at the same

time denying me the reality of that connection. It was like a touch, a light touch of connection, immediately withdrawn. This was the first indication that I was not allowed access to my own records; the letters belonged to my *mother*? But they had been written to Father Hudson's – how could they still belong to *her*?

I looked at the letter about milk tokens, but I couldn't read my mother's writing. He knew I couldn't read; this was a strange token gesture implying trust without truly giving it. But it was something from her. It was her writing. Then Father Tucker shifted focus again. He offered me the letter that I had sent Father Coyne from the Assessment Centre, written in red crayon.

Was this supposed to show that I could not in fact remember my own life, but had to be reminded of it through documentation?

There was a pause. "Your mother had applied to go to South Africa," he said, "then we lost contact with her."
I thought to myself "I've lost her now." Was that slight touch of connection dead for good?

"You came into Care," he went on, "because you were not considered part of the family……."

I went down the stairs and out, and walked back to the Home. It was dark now; I sat on the wall by the school yard and cried and thought my mother was a slut and felt very lost.

I was in shock for some time. But I continued to work at school; things went along normally; I didn't break down or throw tantrums. A month later I came again to the window of Father Tucker's office and knocked. He opened it up: I asked if I could clean his car again. He knew the issue must have been preying on my mind. We spoke briefly about it. There was a pause.
"You took that well." The matter was never discussed again.

Some weeks later when I was cleaning in the chapel, I saw him saying the Office, a form of prayer that priests use every day. I interrupted him to ask "Could I be adopted now?"

"No."
"Why not?"
"That was not what your mother wished."
"Would you get me some rich people?"
"Why?"
"Rich because I want to be able to go out with them, like the others."

Some of the other children went out at weekends with families. Why not me? Was there something odd about me, or did the nuns just have favourites, I wondered? The same children who went out for the weekend were the ones who were picked for carol singing at Christmas time and went to other parties outside the home. I felt singled out in some way as being 'the bad boy'. That's a difficult belief to get rid of.

After that conversation, a Mrs. Riddle used to come over to see me once a week for about a year; she was supposed to help teach me to read and write. It was embarrassing because the other kids were around all the time and I didn't want to read aloud in front of them. She spent most of the time talking to Sister Xavier about her husband, and how he didn't go to mass. I never went out as the others did; only on one occasion did I go to her home, for a weekend. This was the first time that I ever remembered that I had been in a private house. It was a very strange experience. I slept upstairs in a bedroom all by myself, which I had never done before. There was a lounge, and the kitchen was close by, which seemed to me peculiar; the kitchen in Father Hudson's was miles away from the day-room. Mrs Riddle had some children, much younger than me. I was 14 now, and they were only little. They too thought I was very odd: "Why is he in Care? What's he done wrong?" "He's done nothing wrong," she said. "Be quiet."

I felt quite pleased when she stopped coming; she seemed like part of the institution rather than part of the outside world.

One day I was doing a reading test with one of the teachers, Mrs Smith (whom I later knew as Avril), when I burst into tears. The double whammy of finding and then re-losing my family, and the frustration of still not being able to read fluently was more than I could bear. She recognized the strength of my feelings of rejection, failure and isolation. Avril Smith understood my circumstances, and she defended me against the headmaster when he wrote in a school report that I 'had a chip on my shoulder'. She was a kind lady with a certain amount of 'middle-age spread' and curly blondish hair. Sometimes she lost her temper and shouted at us, but by and large we knew that she had our interests at heart.

By this time it had dawned on me that although there was sometimes discussion about moving people back into ordinary mainstream school, the headmaster didn't want to take the risk. So, knowing that I was not going to get any qualifications, the remaining part of my education was simply 'going through the motions'. But Avril Smith took a genuine interest in me and my life. She understood that it might be expected that I would be traumatised by rejection, and she treated me as a human being.

Together with another teacher, Bob Waterhouse, she negotiated with Father Tucker for permission to take me out for a weekend. I went to her house and stayed there with her family several times. This was the first time I ever had the feeling of true acceptance. This was not like staying with Mrs Riddle; I was relaxed. Her two children treated me exactly like other people who stayed in their house. Her husband was a laid-back character who accepted me for what I was.

Presently Avril Smith made a formal request that I should be allowed to come on holiday with her and her family. We went to a trout farm in mid-Wales. We stayed in a farmhouse. The trout were kept in big square ponds dotted around the fields. There was a hatchery where the tiny trout hatched; every morning herons perched above them and the farmer would frighten them away with a shotgun. There was a huge lake nearby next to a hotel; the coloured lights of the hotel shone on the lake at night. If it was calm you could go out on the lake in a rowing boat and see the trout coming up for food. It felt like freedom.

Previously, holiday trips to Penmaenmawr had been my only experience of this other world. Father Hudson's society owned a large house there, right by the sea. Various institutions used it throughout the year. It held about sixteen of us, as well as having room for the nuns, but only one bathroom, as was standard in those days. From the top window you could see the sea. Behind the house were hills, and on the top of one a mini-henge; a stone circle dating from prehistoric times. While we were climbing the hills, the nuns would go for a secret swim, changing in the chalet where we kept our buckets and spades. These were happy times; we had bacon and eggs for breakfast cooked by Sister Francis, and we never wanted the day to end. We swam; we walked to Conway Bay along the beach and looked at the castle. We had picnics on the beach, and we were even allowed to buy an ice cream or try our luck with the one-armed bandits in the amusement arcade. The nun in charge used to bring the pocket money that we had saved throughout the year in her black bag, all sorted into little plastic bags from the bank, full of halfpennies and pennies. If you carried her bag for her it felt like carrying a brick. I never got three lemons in a row in the arcade, so I felt like a right lemon myself. The experience put me off gambling for life.

We didn't have to do our regular cleaning tasks, and we slept in bunk beds instead of our familiar dormitories; it was a total break from our institutional routine and the closest we ever got to 'normal life'. These were the happiest times of my whole life at Father Hudson's.

Apart from visiting Avril Smith, there were occasional breaks in the routine at St Edward's. Bob Waterhouse, who taught us woodwork and who taught me to play the guitar in the afternoon break-time, was a friend of hers. We used to go to a youth club once a week, and he would give me a lift back to the Home, and we would play table tennis in the hall. This also helped to break the boundaries between the institutionalized world of Father Hudson's and the outer world for me.

After the holiday with Avril Smith and her family, I moved up from her class to Mr Tissington's. A slim grey-haired pipe-smoker, he was deputy head. I don't know if it was him or me, but from then on I felt I was just going through the motions at school. There was no suggestion that any of us would take any public exams like O-level or CSE, not even in woodwork or cookery. So lessons were spent in practising how to fill in forms; DHSS forms, driving licence applications, housing benefit forms; they seemed to be endless. We practised mock interviews and we practised how to use the telephone. All this was aimed at preparing us for the outside world, but it was preparing us for very low status and achievement in that world. Meanwhile I was slowly struggling through 'A Tale of Two Cities', which was more interesting. Mr Tissington spotted me reading this. Later, in my end of year report, he wrote, 'He reads books that are above his head'.

But he must have had some feeling that all was not as it should be.
I spent my last day at school gardening. I was putting the spade away and talking to him for the last time.
"You should never have been at this school," he said.
I thought to myself, '*it's too late to tell me that now.*' He was the victim of the system as much as I was.

Chapter Four

At Easter time 1978, I was to leave the Home to go to St. Vincent's, the hostel set up in Birmingham for working boys. On my last day at Father Hudson's, I was upstairs thinking about my mother. Worrying about the outside world I talked to my nun. "Don't bother about them," she said, "they've done nothing for you, but I can't judge them." Then I remember driving over to St Vincent's with Father Tucker in the car, crying. "If it's any consolation your House-mother was crying too." The rest of the journey was spent in silence until we got to St. Vincent's. I was leaving behind everything I knew and embarking on new life. I had no idea what to expect, except that now I would have to earn my own living.

The setting of St Vincent's was in stark contrast to the pleasant countryside of Father Hudson's. There I was, slap bang in the middle of Birmingham, in the middle of traffic noise, the fumes of diesel and factories, in a large building smelling of socks. I had a room which I shared with Paul Wright, and next door was Paul Steers; our little gang of three, all from Father Hudson's. So at least there were familiar faces.

Mr Devine was our Housemaster. A tall, well built bloke with grey hair and a light olive skin, he wore National Health glasses, and was in charge of the whole Working Boys Hostel, as St Vincent's was called. It was a Catholic establishment; mass was compulsory on Sundays at the local church, and local Catholic connections meant I was given a job at S. Rose and Co., working in the dispatch department. This meant spending eight hours a day on my feet, packing clothes and things such as lampshades, clocks and 'fancy items' into cardboard boxes and big brown paper bags. It was tedious in the extreme. I walked there and back every day. I could not afford the bus fare, as I was paid £19.50 a week, and of this £10 went on our keep, and £2.50 was taken as 'compulsory savings', so I only had £7 left to buy clothes and fags. Several other old boys from Father Hudson's worked there too. The whole set up was Victorian in essence. Effectively my whole social circle consisted of ex-Father Hudson inmates.

This move was all a tremendous shock. I had left Father Hudson's with no qualifications, which was very common at that time. It was not the original intention of Father Hudson himself to condemn boys to dead-end jobs, but that is what had happened to me. Mr Devine and Tony Nolan were both old boys of Father Hudson's, so they regarded this system as normal. My background at the Special School made it clear to Mr Devine that I was educationally subnormal, so that a completely mindless and menial job would suit me well.

St Vincent's was intended to prepare you for independent life; you could stay there until you were 18, and then you were turfed out either to find your own 'digs', or to find a flat in one of the housing associations with which they had links. We were not taught to cook; Alban, who worked as a DJ in his spare time, cooked our supper and made our sandwiches for work. The food was much better than at Father Hudson's, and there was more of it, but it would have been more helpful if we had learned to cook it ourselves. Everybody was known as 'Jimmy' this or 'Jimmy' that, which destroyed our identity; I was 'Jimmy Bicknell'. It was I think rather like being in the Army. We were woken every morning by a shout of 'Hands off cocks, on socks!' It was an immensely depressing place to live, and I detested it. The grounds were very small; I intensely missed the space of Father Hudson's, the quietness of it and the sound of the bells on Sunday, and happy memories of the surrounding countryside, the smell of mown grass, cricket, and making houses out of straw bales after the harvest of the surrounding fields.

Homesick and lonely, working in a dead end job with no prospect of change, I was also anxious about where I would go when I was 18.

One evening in 1978, when I had been at St Vincent's for about seven or eight months, Mr Divine the House Master came in to my bedroom: "Father Tucker on the 'phone for you." I came down the corridor to the telephone and picked it up: "Hello?"

"Your grandmother rang from hospital," said Father Tucker, "and she asked me to wish you a Happy Christmas. She said that she was wondering how you were getting on and I said fine".

He sounded friendly, calm, reassuring, encouraging. But this was a blow, a shock. How could he sound like that? I knew I had a family, because Father Tucker had told me about them. I thought about it. This seemed as if it might be building up to something; another contact, perhaps? "Thank you", I said, "good bye".

I thought to myself 'my mother will contact me soon.' I would never have been told about this phone call, I thought, if there was not going to be further development. Why did my grandmother just send a message to wish me a Happy Christmas if she didn't want to speak to me herself?

Christmas came and went; my seventeenth birthday came and went. There was no follow-up to the phone call, and I was left in limbo, waiting.

Then one evening in February I came home from work at six, had my tea as usual and went down to watch the television. One of the boys said "Father Tucker wants to speak to you on the phone." I went upstairs to the phone. "Hello?" Listening, I somehow felt I knew what he was going to say.

"Your mother rang today and said that if you wanted to contact her you can give her a ring at seven o'clock. Only if you wanted to, and she left her number with me for you." "Yes, what's her telephone number?" He gave it to me. I had some problems with writing it down because I had no pen.

So this was to be my decision.

It was some time later that I rang because one of the other boys was using the 'phone.

My mother answered. "Hello, who's speaking please?" She spoke in a deep, soft voice and seemed relaxed. I was numb. But for the first time I felt connected to my umbilical cord - and I wanted to get away from her. *'Oh no it's you!'* I thought. *'I remember you!'* A picture of her came into my mind; not very tall, very strong, blonde. I was flooded with an uncontrollable mix of emotions. I had flashbacks. Suddenly I was a little child again. I remembered the horror of her, and the cruelty. But at some level I loved her, and I thought *'maybe she's changed.'* Unable to get away from the 'phone, I felt I had known her all my life; I felt very close to her, knowing what she was like.

"Karl?" "You're very quiet, you'll have to speak up, I can't hear you," I said. It was a very frightening overwhelming experience; something like being stung by a wasp, but much much worse. I listened to hear the other members of the family in the background, but they weren't there. I felt she was still shutting me out from the rest of the family; this was all of a piece with what she and my father had been doing all these years – they had never sent me a picture of my family, never a Christmas card, never a birthday card. No contact of any kind, until now, and suddenly here was contact; this was my mother, this was a connection. This was her voice. I heard a train go past.

"No", I said, "I'm just listening, do you believe in God?" I wondered if this central belief of mine might be something that we shared; it seemed very important to know, maybe it could be a point of contact. "Yes. I suppose you must have had it drummed in to you there. Umm ....you have three brothers and a sister." "I know."
"Oh! How do you know?"
"Father Tucker told me. This place is like Fort Knox, you couldn't get in contact with me unless the social worker wanted you to. Do the others know about me?"
"No. Francine remembers you, and Sean will. Steven was very little and Paul wasn't born. Do you have a good memory of when you were little?"
"No. Have you got a photograph of me when I was little?" "No," she said, because we've moved around a lot." Was this true, I wondered?

(A flashback to the playroom, looking at photographs of the old boys in the Home at Christmas, and there being no cards from my family, thinking *'when am I going home?')*

"The others have good memories," she said, "of when they were little".
"I can remember being in the pram and a big dog throwing me into the water, I suppose that's why I can't swim." "John can't swim, or read or write."

I must have got that disability from him, I thought; so that's where it comes from.

"When Francine was born your father was like a dog with two tails. John loves kids, I hate them. He would take you all out in the pram". She talked as if to a stranger, relating a story about her life and times; as if she had no connection with me, her son. She rattled on, jumping erratically from one theme to another. Suddenly she flipped back to memories of our babyhood. "You all went up in weight pound by pound when you were born. Francine was six and a half pounds, you were seven and a half, and the little one was ten

and a half. I got the phone in because when the children were little they were ill. When you were born you had pneumonia and Francine got over it quicker than you; you were born too soon. I'm thirty-nine now, I'd got post-natal depression after you were born and I thought I was going to have a breakdown. Your father would never hit you."
I thought to myself, '*I know that.*'

I also had a flashback of myself having pneumonia; but not as a baby, as a little boy of eight or nine, in the dormitory. I remembered it seemed to take weeks to recover; I remembered my hot water bottle bursting in my bed, and lying in a puddle. I was afraid at the time to tell Sister Xavier in case she thought I had wet the bed and I would have to go all the way down to the bathroom, and to the laundry with my wet sheets.

Post-natal depression afflicts many women, and many of them do in fact reject their children. It was a plausible explanation for what she had done to me. Now, I think it was an explanation she could live with.

On she went: "Your father didn't have a very good mother. She rang last week; she didn't care if you were down there. It would have been much worse for you if you had stayed; what I did was best. Your father didn't understand. I would throw his clothes out of the window to stop him going to work, because I couldn't bear to be alone, and he would put you all in the other room if we were having an argument."
I remembered suddenly how frightening their rows had been.
"He came when I was nine," I said.
"He shouldn't have done that."
'*Why not?*' I thought to myself.
"I divorced him in 1974." "I know." "I divorced him because of his drinking; he can drink twenty pints a night. I get on with him sometimes; I think he's a bit of a schizophrenic. We were having an argument one day and he threw a pan of boiling water over the dog and it ran away. I think he is a male chauvinist pig."
"Did you ever come up to see me?" "No. I had to go to Stratford once because I had problems having the last one." (Stratford was in Warwickshire; I suppose that was as near as she got to me.)
"How old was I when I came into Care?"
"Four and a half."

"Father Tucker said eighteen months!"

Now who was I to believe?

"My mother was in the hospital having an operation and we were talking about you. She's two-faced. I hated my own father, he died of cancer. I wished at the time they would have given him something to get him out of the pain.... how tall are you?"
"About five feet nine."
"You're as tall as the next one down from you. I'm five feet two, I'm small. I've got a little dog here, I suppose if you're small you like small things. What colour are your eyes?"
"Blue with green."
"I've got green eyes. Maybe I will come up to see you in the summer."

We spoke for an hour on the 'phone before she said:
"I'll have to stop talking because it's expensive to ring you from Cardiff. I'll send you a photograph of us when I can get round to it."
We said goodbye. After I had put the receiver down, at first I felt happy that she had called, thinking to myself *'maybe it's time for her to accept me now',* but still not really knowing what she was like.

Ultimately she left me feeling let down. *'It's too late now,'* I thought, *'I've missed out after all this time.'*
I thought *'she's lying'.* Then I rang Father Tucker. "Hello."
"My mother was telling me that she hated kids and that I was born too soon."
"Do you think if you were a girl she would have accepted you?"
The question made me feel uneasy about him so I didn't answer it.

It was supper time and I was talking to Mr. Divine.
"Mothers get in contact just to get your money," he said, "because you're working." I knew this attitude was very common, but I thought, *'I know she didn't contact me for that.'*

That same night I lay in bed in my room thinking *'I'm having a breakdown.'* It was as if I was talking to myself. I couldn't sleep for thinking of my mother; I masturbated. And then I lay thinking *'this is wrong,'* and feeling so guilty – but somehow I just loved her and just wished I was there the way she described the others to me. I felt so much on the outside. Thinking that Shaun had taken my place, I felt so jealous of him and imagined myself fighting him. Over the next week I was just in a dreamy state, mostly sitting in my room, and for the first time in my life I started fidgeting with my hair. (That became a compulsive habit for me for years to come.) I must stop that, I thought to myself. I had lost my appetite, and wrote my family's names on pieces of paper over and over again. Sometimes I felt quite high and happy and other times down and dejected. Will she ever accept me? I talked to myself as if another member of my family were there with me. I felt disgusted with myself and wanted to change my name.

At that point I wanted to disassociate myself from the whole experience of this connection with my mother. I thought back to the Assessment Centre and realised '*this is what that was all about*'. I realised that my early rejection must have led to the behaviour which took me to the psychiatrist. I felt that I was quite mad, and then I wondered, '*would I ever do to any woman what my mother had done to me?*'. I knew that the basic understanding of abuse was that if you have been abused, you are likely to abuse. The thought terrified me, and it took me years to unravel this belief.

It was as if I had been kept in a dark room for years and suddenly someone was shining a brilliant searchlight on me. I felt as if I had been brutally exposed; raped even. And I felt so guilty. I couldn't talk to anybody about this. From being a reasonably extroverted person, suddenly I imploded into a self conscious wreck.

Chapter Five

The following week my impatience got the better of me and I went to see Father Tucker again.
"I've lost my mother's telephone number. Could I ring from the office?"
"Yes."
My mother answered the 'phone.
"Hello, who's speaking please?"
"Karl."
I could hear my brothers in the background and the tone of their voices was just like mine.
"The next time you want to ring would you ask the priest?"

This door was closed to me then? And if so, why? Was this to be an 'appointment only' kind of contact? I suspected that my brothers and sisters didn't know of my existence yet.
"Your father was saying that if you were down here you would be just like the others, into Status Quo and all that."
No, I thought, I can't stand them actually.
"I can't call you Mum."
"I know that."
"Are you going to tell the others?"
"Paul, the little one, does impersonations" - he was doing one of his teachers; I could hear him in the background.
'He's just like me.' I thought.
"Paul had told me that Francine got home from a night club late. Your father doesn't like tell-tales, he said he'd hit him so Paul ran upstairs and John ran after him into his room and swore at him."
'It all seems like fun', I thought.
"Could I speak to him?"
"Your father won't come to the 'phone at all, ever. If he's ill, I even have to ring his work place up for him."

It was tea time so we both said our goodbyes.
I went home on the bus thinking to myself, *'Why don't the other members of the family know about me?'*
Some days later I smashed my record player, then sat down and started to cry.

I rang my mother's number the following week without asking the priest; I had felt suspicious of him on the day I'd made the telephone call in his office.
"Hello, who's speaking please?"
"Karl."
"Who?" in a surprised voice.
"You know, Karl Bicknell."
"No, my mother's out, she goes out on Thursday, how are you?"
"Fine." It was my sister, Francine. She sounded slightly shocked.

On Sunday morning I rang up again.
"Hello."
"Who am I speaking to?
"Stefan."
"Did you know you have another brother?" I asked. Then I put the telephone down. I got on the bus out to Coleshill, feeling very uneasy about what I had done. When I got home in the evening one of the boys said
"There's been a woman on the phone all day asking for you."

The phone rang. It was my mother.
"Have you got the telephone number of that priest?"
I gave it to her and the phone went dead.

The following day I went off to Coleshill and spoke to Father Tucker. "She's just trying to work off her guilty feelings," he said. "She should have told them. It would have been better if she had told them. They were bound to ask. And what else hasn't she told us? She said that you were steamrolling it, why didn't you talk to me about it?"

I gave no reply. I could hear him saying to himself, "here's the root of the rejection. You weren't loved there, you were loved here; we didn't teach you to lash out at others."

I asked him if he had spoken to my father about it.
"Yes," he said. "Your mother said they did not want the other children to know in case it would make them feel unwanted. If you carry on like that you might lose contact. Two or three meetings will trigger off an acceptance. If that's what you want, to be returned to the bosom of the family, give that wound time to heal. She will have to accept you first, and then bring the rest

of the family round." I got home that evening and one of the boys said "Father Tucker rang Mr Divine." *'I bet that's about my mother'* I thought. So I was being discussed.

I rang her up late some days later.
"Do the others know?"
"No, why bring them into this. Your father said that if you were down here he would have hit you. He thinks it's better that they don't know."
I thought about what he had said at Coleshill when he came up; *'So he's turned his back on me, too.'*

"Father Tucker said you feel guilty," said my mother on our next contact.
"I don't feel guilty. Is my father my father?"
"I can't say that over the 'phone, I can't talk to you now." We said our goodbyes and I put the 'phone down.

Chapter Six

Soon after this I found that I was becoming more distanced from the children that I had grown up with. So I moved from St Vincent's to live with a family, to experience what family life was like. Father Tucker knew some people and I went to live with them.

By now it was the 1980s.   John and Mary Murter lived in Handsworth Wood; they were Catholics with a large family. He was an architect and she was a teacher. It was a large Victorian house, and I had a small bedroom on the top floor. This was the first time that I had lived outside an institution, but it was an unconventional household. All the children were very clever; one played the piano, another was interested in politics; it was a big change for me. I stayed in contact with my mother, but it was a very strained connection. I learned from her that my sister Francine had moved out of home to work in a hospital, so I gave a ring there.

"You've been a very naughty boy, it was like a madhouse that day when you rang Stefan" said Francine. "I was wondering what was going on all those years ago, when I was little." As I was speaking the phone went dead.

I rang my mother up. "Hello." "Haven't you any pen friends?" "No."
"You're just trying to break your way in through Francine. She said that you rang her up at the hospital and she said that if you keep ringing up she is going to leave. Scientists say that women sometimes do reject their offspring. I'd have thought by now you would've understood, I just wish I could turn back the clocks. Don't ring up here again." Then she hung up.

Some time later Father Tucker came to do his last assessment of me, unbeknownst to me. I didn't like the idea of him coming. I walked into the Murters' sitting room, and he was sitting there, alone. I didn't want to talk to him about my mother saying I was not to ring her up again. I felt deeply uncomfortable in his presence, as if I had done something terribly wrong. I hadn't used him as a go-between because I didn't trust him any longer.

Some weeks later he sent my full birth certificate through the post. That showed my father as John Bicknell, face-miner, and my mother as Georgina Kathleen Francesca, formerly Pasticcio, audio typist. This was reassuring; I was not illegitimate after all. But contact with my family was lost. I felt grief,

I mourned, but they were not dead. So I couldn't express this grief in any acceptable way, and there was no way that it could end.

Months passed by. I remained clinically depressed, though nobody recognized this. I lost all interest in life; I didn't turn up for work and got sacked. 'We'll have to let you go,' said Mr Buckler. And things were not working out in the house where I lived; Mr Murter thought I was 'work-shy' and had no idea what I was going through. I started to drink and they asked me to leave. I didn't leave that night, I had nowhere to go. I went round to see a friend the following day. He was a probation officer; I had met him through doing some voluntary work with handicapped people, as they were known then. We both went to the Murters' house, and Mary the older daughter said that I ought to ring up Father Tucker as he agreed that I ought to be kicked out and said that I needed help. I didn't ring him, and I didn't go back, but with the probation officer's help I found another place. I moved to Plunkett House. Now the Archbishop's house, it was a hostel in those days, and I stayed there for about a year.

Chapter Seven

By now I was 19; it was 1981. One day I went up from Plunkett House to Coleshill to see Sister Xavier.
"Do you ever hear anything from your mother?" she asked. "No."
Then we talked about other things. I didn't want to talk about my family.

I met Father Tucker the same day in his office, and we talked. "Sometimes fantasy helps us cope with reality," I said. I meant that the shock of reconnection with my family had been so great that I sometimes retreated into the fantasy that it had never really happened. I knew this was fantasy, but it was still helpful. "Yes," he replied. I felt reassured; maybe he empathized with my feelings. Maybe there was some rapport here, after all.

I showed him a piece of paper that someone had given me where I worked. It was a puzzle. On one side was the statement: "on the reverse is the truth" and on the other side was written: "on the reverse is a lie". This puzzle had appealed to me because I felt so confused about the truth. Who knew what? At what age had I come into Father Hudson's? Why would my mother say one thing and Father Tucker another? We talked about the puzzle; this was an indirect way of talking about my own life.

"Well the one cancels out the other" said Father Tucker. This didn't help very much. "So what happened with your mother?"
"You gave me her telephone number, at St. Vincent's, over the 'phone."
"No, she rang you", he said.
"No."
"You came up here to ring from my office."
"That was because I lost the number a week later," I argued. He didn't reply.

He seemed to be trying to get me to admit that any sort of breakdown in contact with my family was entirely my own fault. I couldn't accept this. I was a lad of 17 when he suggested I could call my mother. I had been given no advice about how to handle such a call; I had been given no support of any kind afterwards. I had felt overwhelming emotions of guilt about the way I had made the contact, and the way it had ended so abruptly. I had been in a terrible and destructive mental loop from which I had not been able to escape or recover for months. My self-esteem had plummeted; the whole experience had effectively caused me to break down. And living at Plunkett

House didn't help matters; it was intended for elderly people and was very depressing. My personality had changed. I couldn't argue with him about all this, so I chose the most immediate problem; my housing.

"You had me kicked out of the Murters," I accused.
"Who told you that? If you tell me I'll let you know if it's the truth."
Why couldn't he tell me the truth anyway? Why did this have to be a bargain? I said nothing.
"I will have to break this off now," he said, and walked out of the room. I was left sitting there, realizing that if I didn't agree with everything he said, all 'rapport' was at an end. This was devastating. This was the man I had trusted all through my adolescence, and now here he was failing to support me in any way.

Presently Plunkett House closed down, greatly to my relief. The housing association connected to it found me a flat in Handsworth. For the first time I was independent; I liked this. Several other ex-Hudson's boys lived in the area too, so I at least there were some people that I knew around me.

I began to recover some self confidence. I got a job in Hockley jewellery quarter in Birmingham. It had its own police force, and a college where you could study gemology, goldsmithwork and jewellery design. I was what used to be called a 'jobber' which involved repairing jewellery. I enjoyed all this and began to recover somewhat.

Presently I remembered that my grandmother had rung to wish me a happy Christmas, and I felt the whole situation was still completely unresolved, so I rang Father Tucker.
"Do you have the address of my grandmother with you?"
"Yes."
"If I write to her will you pass it on?"
"Yes, I will do that for you."
"Thank you."
I put the 'phone down.

I wrote to my grandmother, and sent the letter to Father Tucker for him to forward. I simply introduced myself, told her where I lived and what I was doing, and sent her my best wishes. It was a big effort to write that letter; I used dictionary and tried to keep my dyslexic handwriting as clear as I could.

Some weeks later my grandmother wrote back on blue paper. The handwriting was not much better than mine, and her grammar was worse. The letter was quite overwhelming. She was all over me, asking me to live with her. I wrote back in a detached way, thinking of what happened with my mother years before. "I will come to see you soon after I get back from France," I wrote.

Presently I met up with some of the Little Sisters of Jesus. This was an order inspired by Charles de Foucauld, who wanted to devote his life to living with the poorest of the poor in the inner cities. Tragically he was killed before fulfilling this ambition, but it was realized later by others. I went with them to a Taizé weekend in Cradley, where I met up with the local vicar and his wife. They used to have me to stay for weekends, which was great; it was a way to get out of the city, which basically I loathed. The experience of the Taizé weekend triggered off a childhood ambition to travel.

Taizé is in mid-France, and the Taizé movement is an international ecumenical movement founded by Frère Roger. Some of the brothers live and work in Taizé itself and others are scattered across the world.

Presently I went to Taizé on my own. I got a ticket to Paris, and then hitchhiked through France. This was freedom. I didn't speak a word of French; I bought a map, and made a sign saying 'Macôn', which I held up as I walked along. I got lifts from lorry drivers; if they didn't speak English it was a silent ride. I was completely shattered by the time I got there, and spent about ten days there before hitching back. This was where I met Andreas Fisher-Barnacle. He was the son of a professor in Heidelberg, and was working at Taizé for the summer holidays. He spoke American English, as well as his native German. All around me people were speaking different languages and translating and interpreting for each other. This was a great experience. In the daytime there were talks and discussions, prayers and singing of the Taizé liturgy; some in Latin, some in German, some in French, some in Spanish, English, Italian. Sometimes the translations were not strictly accurate; 'Magnificat' used to be sung as 'I've got a cat, I've got a cat, it's called Maria; dominoes', etc by some of the English element. For the first time I was starting to launch out by myself, into a world which was not bounded by Father Hudson's.

I made friends, but my experience in care had left me with a sense of awkwardness which other people, at least on the surface, didn't seem to have. One of my talents is to be able to mimic accents and voices very accurately; this won friends easily and made them laugh. But there was still a sense of separation from other people.

After I came back from France I hitch-hiked to Stratford to see my grandmother. I found the cottage where she lived and knocked on the door. A man opened it.

"Hello, my name's Karl. Have I got the right house? I'm looking for Mrs. Pasticcio."
"Yes", said the man, "I'm Larry, I'm your grandmother's husband."
He called up the stairs and my grandmother came down wearing dark sunglasses. She was a small woman with black hair, and the moment I saw her it hit me straight in the stomach.
'I remember you', I thought. I tried to stop myself from crying. She was crying herself. She came over to me and put her hands on my face.

I noticed two small pictures on the mirror. "Who are these people?" "Your grandfather at a wedding, and my son Steven."
Then we walked into the front room and sat ourselves down.
"The Father has written a nice letter to me."

I did not understand what she was talking about so I said nothing. Then she got herself a drink out of the cabinet next to where she was sitting. Thinking of my father I didn't like to see her do that, but I said nothing.

She seemed very happy and rang my 'Uncle Victor'. This was my grandmother's son, brother to my mother, and to Steven and Maria, I learned.
"Have a guess who's here? It's Karl!"
Still in a weepy state she gave me the 'phone.
"Here, talk a little."
I didn't know what to say to him.
"If you're ever down in Cardiff come and see us," he said.

Having my dinner that evening I felt a little shocked by it all. "You look like your brother Stefan. Francine was nice when she was little, but then she changed."

She talked about the family, and I felt so outside of it all. "Where were your parents from?"
"My mother was from Norway and my father was Spanish," she said, waving her arms in the air.
"What was your marriage like?" I asked boldly.
"JoJo, your grandfather, was an Italian. We were very close," she said, putting her arms around herself. "He died of cancer. When he was dying he said to me, "don't worry, Karl will look after you when I die."

"What was my mother like as a child?" "She was a tomboy. One Christmas your mother wanted a gun," she said, and she laughed. *She laughs just like my mother*, I thought. She talked about my uncles and aunts and what they were like. "Your grandfather would say to your mother 'has someone stood on your nose?' because he had a big nose and she had a nose a bit like his." She laughed again.
"What was my father's father like?"
"He was a very humble man, and his mother was a very bombastic person."
I thought of what my mother had said and I didn't like the sound of her.

Soon after we had finished chattering I went for a walk all around Stratford before coming back to the house. "You walk just like your father," remarked my grandmother. I didn't like the thought of being like my father.

Then we watched "Hi-de-Hi" and she told me how she had worked in a holiday camp. That's where she met Larry, Larry the Lamb as she would call him. I was quite tired after all the travelling over the last few days, so I went to bed. It was a strange feeling, being in my grandmother's house.

The following day I got the bus home. Feeling detached from her, not wanting to get hurt, I said "Goodbye grandmamma," and she laughed. "I will come up see you again."
Yes, I would go and see her when I could.

One day over in Stratford, we had another chat.

"I said to your mother 'Do you want to get married?' and she said 'Yes.' 'Marriage isn't a bunch of roses,' I said 'but you made your bed so lie in it.' So I told them to get out. She kept running round to me saying 'It's Karl.' It was so awful; your mother would put you in a room and feed you with scraps of bread. Sometimes you don't want to know."

I realized what this story meant....
"I told them to go to counselling about their marriage," she went on, "but they didn't go. John couldn't read, so your mother got someone to give him some reading lessons, but he didn't stick to them."

Over at Stratford another day we were talking in the front room. "When I die I will leave everything to you." Looking around the room I thought to myself, *'she has nothing to leave'.* Larry had told me that the furniture was bought on hire purchase; maybe she was trying to keep a hold on me.

Later that evening in a wine bar she was trying to get me drunk by pouring her wine into my glass. She said "You're very stand-offish, why don't you bring your friends over?" I didn't answer her but just went on drinking the wine. "You're a very intelligent person," she said.

I couldn't tell her that she embarrassed me. She would go round Stratford drunk, saying to people, "He's my grandson."

One night she'd telephoned my mother to say that I was gay. I thought that my mother was right when she said that my grandmother was two-faced but I couldn't help myself feeling sorry for her, she seemed so lonely. One day after we'd been to the supermarket I was trying to stop her buying a bottle of cider. When we got home she screamed, "I want you to go, you bastard!" I was shocked by the tone of her voice. I left, and then thought of going back, but in the end I didn't.

I thought for a long time that I would never get married; *'this thing stops here with me.'* I would go over and over the telephone conversations in my mind and wish I had never picked up the 'phone in the first place.

Chapter Eight

After this encounter I decided to go abroad again, for a longer trip. By this time it was 1982. My job in the jewellery quarter had come to an end; Britain was in the grip of a recession, Handsworth had rioted, and there was nothing to keep me. I bumped into an old friend, Paul Steers, who was now living in Holland. I thought I would try to make a clean break and see how long I could last in Europe.

I bought a book called 'Work your Way Around Europe', and another called 'A Hitch-hikers Guide to Europe', and set off. I left all my possessions in a friend's barn near Malvern, and I knew that when I came back I could stay in London for a while. I was in my early twenties now, and the world outside Britain seemed like freedom. I wanted to explore that new world; a world outside Father Hudson's, on my own. And I wanted to explore myself, too.

So I bought a return ticket for the ferry to Belgium (just in case!) and set off. I reached Brussels, and went from there to Holland. The two books I had bought became my bibles; they told me where to eat and where to stay, and where to find seasonal work. In Holland, after getting down to my last few guilders and sleeping on the pavement I eventually found work trimming tulip bulbs. This was cripplingly hard work and very boring, but I managed to learn a bit of Dutch (children taught me to swear!) and spent a weekend in Amsterdam, exploring. Once I borrowed a bike and rode to the sea to have a look round. Then I lost the bike; panic. I walked around for hours, looking in every street. I found it in the end.

The sense of freedom was exhilarating. It was hard to believe that I was actually here, on my own, surviving. I was amused by the other travellers, and I found that I had a whole year of what you might call 'railway conversations' - travel talk. "Hi, where are you from? Where have you been so far? Oh, really, what was that like?" etc. The Australians seemed to aim to spend at least a year traveling around, but they seemed more independent than the Americans, who used to send their socks home to be washed.

The tulip job came to an end, and I went back to Brussels, and in twenty four hours had found myself a job in the floor service of the Royal Windsor Hotel, opposite the station, for the whole of August. I worked in the afternoons, from 2.00 until late at night, fetching champagne, sandwiches, coffee, etc, and found I could make up to 800 francs a day; people tipped generously. A bucket of ice delivered to the executive suite would usually result in a tip of 100 Belgian francs; a lot of money then.

I lived in the Brussels youth hostel, which was against the rules, but nobody seemed to mind. I never had to answer the phone in the hotel, and many of the guests spoke English, so language was not a problem.

Then I set off to Luxembourg, where I lost my wallet. Thirteen thousand Belgian francs, gone. I was destitute again. I rang friends in London, who wired me £50, of which the bank took £10, naturally. I decided to go and see my friend Andreas in Heidelberg; maybe I could stay with him for a while and get some work grape-picking? I got there; I found him. He introduced me to another friend, who in turn introduced me to another, who offered me some work restoring a baroque house in Heidelberg. Heidelberg is picture-postcard beautiful, plus it has one of the oldest universities in Germany.

I worked on this house for three or four months, painting and labouring, pushing the wheelbarrow, stripping off plaster etc. While I was there I read 'A picture of Dorian Grey', and 'I'm OK, You're OK'. I picked this up quite by chance in a bookstall. This was my first encounter with therapy or analysis of any kind, and it was very interesting. I began to analyse myself in the context of this model; was I a 'contaminated adult?' This was quite scary. Which part of the model did I fit into? I went back to the encounter with my mother and tried to think it through.

When the job was done, I went back to Taizé for a while. By this time it was Christmas, and the Taizé centre was having a big international meeting in Paris, so I went there.

At the meeting I met Marie Dominique, a kindergarten teacher. We clicked. Presently we went skiing briefly; it was cross-country skiing, which is not too difficult (although I kept falling over), and then parted company. I went to Austria, started to run out of money, and wrote to ask her if I could come back to back to Paris again. She said yes, and there I would stay for another four months, in her little community in Nanterreville, not far from the university where the évènements began in 1968.

For a few weeks I worked for the Socialist Party, handwriting envelopes to be sent out to voters. I was glad of the work, as I was embarrassed to live with these people without being able to pay my way. It was a mixed group; an accountant, a social worker, a teacher….but all were in therapy of some kind. One did psycho-drama, another was in psycho-analysis; some were in group therapy. So it was a supportive group for a young man confused about his own psyche. I began to learn some of the processes; matching body language, for instance, and I realized that good therapy might be a way to resolve internal conflicts. What I didn't realise was that there are not only many different types of therapy which suit different types of people, but that there are therapists and therapists, each with their own agenda.

The encounter with these people, through the Taizé meeting, was an important turning point for me. It was a relief to know that other people had problems; maybe I wasn't alone in having a problematic childhood.

In the end I decided I couldn't live on this group's charity any longer, and that I had better go back to England. Badly-paid farm work didn't appeal.

It was spring. After a year of travelling so freely I hated the thought of living in inner-city Birmingham again so I went to Malvern. I knew Malvern slightly, as I had met the vicar at a Taizé weekend. I stayed with friends for a while until I'd found a room in a house to rent. I did some casual work for a while, and made a week's trip to Denmark.

Back in Malvern, I rang Father Tucker and told him that I was feeling a bit dejected at having to come back to England. Father Hudson's was the closest thing I ever had to family; it felt natural to make contact again.

He made a sarcastic joke about my feelings. "Did you think you were going to come back in great triumph as a hero?" There was a pause. "Don't you want to face the past?" he asked. "Anger distorts the personality." That made me feel very uncomfortable, as if he was holding something over me. "When are you going to come and see me?" I asked. "I don't do round trips these days" he replied. "Why don't you come up here?"

I felt that I was being manipulated again. It all made me flash back again, to the encounter with my mother, and triggered terrible feelings of guilt and inadequacy. I felt compelled in some way to do something about it; maybe anger really was distorting my personality and I should do something about it? But I no longer trusted Father Tucker. I felt I needed to try to resolve the past with somebody unconnected with Father Hudson's; somebody who would have a fresh perspective on my story.

Presently my landlord had to sell his house and I needed a new place to live. I asked around at St Joseph's church in Malvern, and by chance I met a therapist, a Mr Millet, and told him that I felt inadequate about not having a job. He offered me some therapy.

Somewhere along the line I had picked up the adage that 'if you've been abused, you are likely to abuse'. As I have said, this is a seriously disturbing idea; it makes you older than you are. It leads to horrible fear, and it makes you keep your distance from women. It's a heavy burden. It makes you feel *'if I get close to this woman, I may finish up damaging her'.* It puts you off wanting to make relationships; you haven't committed any crime, but you feel guilty all the same. Abuse is a secret which you can't confide to anyone, in case they reject you. So you end up rejecting genuine chances of friendship, let alone close relationships with the opposite sex. And Father Tucker had said, 'anger distorts the personality'. This echoed through my mind. So I felt I had to go into therapy, to rid myself of this unfinished business, and try to free myself from this false guilt, and my fear of the future.

I was able to talk to Mr Millet about Thomas Harris's book, 'I'm OK, You're OK', so he was interested by that and we moved on from there. Soon we were discussing life in Father Hudson's, the disastrous contact with my mother, and the important issue of my legitimacy/illegitimacy. Mr Millet was an Anglican vicar and very well-intentioned. A grey haired man with a rounded face and square glasses, he inspired me with some naïve trust that this methodology was going to work. He had trained in various different therapeutic disciplines; Gestalt therapy, Rebirthing therapy, Carl Rogers' encounter groups and his theories of unconditional acceptance. He conducted these sessions in a room in the church precincts. I attended several sessions.

Presently these discussions triggered off a decision to make contact with my family again. I was still frustrated that my mother hadn't told the family about me. I rang up Cardiff once more.
"Hello."
"Who am I speaking to?"
"Stefan." This was a brother I had never seen; two years younger than myself.
"Can you remember," I asked, "years ago when someone rang you up and said that you had another brother?"
"Yes."
"That was me."
"I found your birth certificate", he said. "Were you adopted?"
"No."
"Do you want to see us?" he asked.
"Yes. My grandmother says that I look like you."
I made some plans to come down and see him, then said goodbye.

Having thought about what my mother had said before, I rang again. "Hello." It was Stefan again who replied.
"I suppose I'm coming in the back door?"
"Yes, my mother was saying something like that."

I came down on the train a week later, and rang from a box in the street when I got there. There was no reply, so I waited on the other side of the street. The family house is a council house which my mother had bought from the council in the 80s; a semi-detached red brick building near the railway line. Looking up I could see my sister's name 'Francine' written in the concrete lintel above the porch.

Stefan appeared with a bicycle wheel in his hand. I instantly knew it was him. He looked familiar; he was taller than me, with dark hair to his shoulders. He recognized me, too; he looked across and said "Karl?" "Yes."

I walked over to him and we both went inside the house and sat down in the kitchen. We talked a little; he was quite gentle I thought, and I liked him. "What was my mother saying?" "She said that when you were born your father left, then she cried and went to bed." "Has he stopped drinking yet?" "Yes, he's never done that much for us, I don't know what he's thinking of."

I told him about my contact with my mother from St. Vincent's, and how I could hear the family all talking in the background, and how the tone of their voices sounded exactly like my own. And about my father not wanting to tell them all about me, and how I smashed my record player. "I bet you did......you look just like Shaun." Shaun was one year younger than me.

It was so very hard for me to be in that house. This was my family yet I felt on the outside of it. "Do you want to see Dad?" I made a gesture with my hand, meaning 'I'm not sure...' "That's just like what Shaun would do" said Stefan again.

He called upstairs to my father, who came down a little later into the kitchen. He had black hair still, but he was an older man now, and I was taller than him. He rubbed his hands together and smiled. I remembered his smile from when I was little, but I couldn't really tell what he was thinking then. I offered him a seat and showed him a picture of my first Holy Communion; "This is about the time you came up to see me."

He looked at it, then got up and moved over to the cooker saying nothing. This was clearly a rejection. Stefan picked up his bicycle wheel and we both went out to the back yard. We shared a joint and he made a joke about the hash trade. He started fixing the wheel to the bike, and we went upstairs. He started to show me photos of other members of the family, and it was true, I **do** look exactly like my brother Shaun...; the only difference between us is that his eyes are light green and mine are blue. He showed me pictures of my sister, Francine. "She was anorexic," said Stefan bluntly, "but she's got over that now. I always thought she was thick, but she went on to be a nurse in Hammersmith hospital."

I found that like the rest of my family, he spoke rather abruptly; it's something that people have said about me, too. Our sense of humour was identical; we laughed at exactly the same things. He remarked that I had loads of cousins, in his Cardiff accent, and told me how Paul (brother number three, two years younger than Stefan) used to do impersonations (just as I can). "He's brainy," said Stefan, 'he's doing electronics at college." The similarities between us all were quite uncanny, like looking in a mirror. Physically, this caused me to feel immense tension; he was the acceptable version, and I was the unacceptable one....I felt as though I might crack, and indeed I did. I wasn't able to control myself and just burst into tears, thinking *'all this time I've known about you and you haven't known about me.'* "Bicknell", Stefan said, and came across and put his arms around me. It was so strange hearing him say that.

He told me that Shaun was in prison. "A lot of petty things caught up with him." "My mother talked to me on the 'phone about his stealing," I said. "He just got in with the wrong people." I talked about the records in the Children's Home saying that I was illegitimate. "That's OK, you're one of us."

All in all this whole meeting was very intense and I did not really know how to handle it. We went downstairs and out of the house. Walking to the train station Stefan started to cry. "How do you feel about all this?" I asked. "I don't know." I didn't know how I felt either, so I said "Remember me", then watched him go, thinking *'I may never see him again'*, and caught the train home.

Chapter Nine

I resumed my counselling sessions with Mr Millet. "I'm not here to tell you what to do with your life," he said. "You have a lot of unfinished business; and how long has this been going on for?"

I gave no reply thinking *'this is strange. What did he mean?'* What I needed was a job, I thought, not simply a lot of self-analysis. I didn't really want to talk about my past - I was skating around the situation. But most therapists are only interested in the client's interior life.

"If you went to see your mother" he said, "all the past would come back and would be too much for her, that would make her feel doubly guilty. So you were rejected. I bet it made you angry that she was blocking you out." Well, yes, it had me feel angry, of course; this was stating the obvious. But to suggest that going to visit her would be in some way cruel to her only made me feel more guilty still for even thinking about it. This was my first experience of therapy, and like many later therapeutic sessions, it made me feel worse, and only seemed to be telling me things I knew already.

The next time I went to Mr Millet he said "Let's work this out here, but only if you want to. Two or three meetings should trigger off an acceptance of you; you may be her salvation." I had heard this before; it acted as a trigger, flooding me with bad bad memories. Also, this particular therapist had a tendency to talk about his own problems, about his daughter's problems, and her rejection of his grandson.... As I listened, I began to feel that he had some empathy with me. On the other hand, I began to wonder if like him, I would still be wrestling with my own problems when I was sixty. It was not very encouraging.

Nevertheless, I thought *'if I can get through this I will be able to get back with my mother and see my brother again.'*

So after some months of therapy I rang Father Tucker up. "I've seen my brother; it was like getting back into the family." "Have you tried to patch things up with your mother?" he asked. "No, I came on too strong with my mother and we just clashed with each other all those years ago." "Oh, is that what it was? Learn to let your anger out more slowly."

Psychotherapy with Hugh Millett proved to be more difficult than I first imagined it would be. I went through a 'rebirthing'. I thought at the time that this therapy was going to resolve everything about my past. He took me through an imagery process. At first things were quite good. It was the strangest experience I've ever had, even to the point that I could smell chloroform in the air. I suppose this was my first memory, I thought that night as I lay peacefully in bed, but as time progressed old symptoms recurred; similar to those that arose on my first contact with my mother.

Over the next few months my fears were coming up again one after another, and I was feeling a great deal of physical tension and paranoia. At times I fell into a deep depression which I could feel physically like pressure on both sides of my temples. At other times I was in a state of mania, laughing hysterically. I interpreted all this as being obviously my mother's mood swings. I'd remember things that I had long forgotten about those early years; not all bad. Does she love me, doesn't she love me? I remembered things about my father coming home from work, and how pleased I was to see him.

In some sessions I used what are called 'empty chairs'; an externalization technique where I would have to imagine my mother sitting on one chair. The fear of this proved to be intensely difficult; the fear that I had was of rejection. In one session Hugh said, "Ah, there's the root of the rejection!"

During this period the pain of re-experiencing my early childhood and my mother's rejection of me caused an intense grief and I couldn't stop crying. It was very difficult for me to connect fully with any of the good experiences of my life. During this constant nagging pain Father Tuckers voice echoed through my head; 'anger distorts the personality'. When will I ever get through this? How long is this going to go on for? Will I ever get better? And will I ever be again be the same person that I was before the contact with my mother?

Each time I went into therapy it was like going to confession. As if I had committed a big sin; but I was never absolved. It reminded me of what had happened when I got in contact with my mother.

During my time in therapy I read a lot about it and wrote my feelings down. I must have spent a whole year just crying and getting more and more miserable, thinking *when is all this going to stop.'* I thought that I would never be able to get over that stage of my life. I read about children who are rejected by their parents (among other things R D Laing, The Divided Self, Knots, Conversations with Children, Burns, Games People Play; I even tried to tackle Sartre's Theory of the Emotions).

The intensity of my feelings mounted and mounted until one day I felt so distraught that I slashed my wrist with a knife. Then I got evicted and found myself homeless. I thought *'this is never going to stop. Everything that I say seems to have to be analyzed.'* It made me feel more exasperated than ever, but I felt that I must go on.

Eventually after a great deal of work in therapy and the reading I had done I began to feel that I had the confidence to confront Father Tucker. I went up to Coleshill; it was a cold winter's day. Father Tucker was just coming over for his dinner. He came into the kitchen. I looked at him; he just stood there, then pulled on his jacket sleeves and moved his head from side to side. Was he just cold, or was this a way of shaking his head? Then he shook his hands, too, and said to the nun, "Is it OK to go down?" "Yes Father."

I followed him down to the Priest's Dining Room. We both walked in and sat down. He poured out some coffee.
"May I have one?"
"Yes."
"I've been to see my brother."
"Did you see your mother?"
"No."
"I did not tell you to do that," reminding me of what he had suggested about the first contact. So he was supposed to be in charge, and I was supposed to be compliant? I was breaking the rules? My mother must accept me before I speak to my own brother?

"You incompetent bastard," I broke out. "What you did to me was horrific; you know that I was rejected, you know rejected children don't trust their parents, they feel fear, anxiety and separation and the self that kills the self. I've been through rebirthing therapy. I've been re-experiencing all the pain of that initial rejection. I've read a lot about this, and you would know this because it's your *job* to know."

"Are you blaming me?" he asked, pointing to himself. "That was your mother," and he pointed upwards, as if my mother was there. I looked up to where his finger was pointing and felt terrified panic. *I know now that this pointing was an NLP technique to disconcert and put you into trance-like state when you are trying to process a great deal of material at once.*

"If I could have had it my way I would have broken the contact off," he said. *'Hold on a minute',* I thought, *'whose family are we talking about here?'* "I'm a Bicknell first and foremost," I said. "No one can deny you that. How much of what you told me about your mental state was true?"

I looked down. From the corner of my eye I could see him just sitting there, his coffee in one hand, moving his head from side to side while his other hand was moving from side to side too. He twitched all over. It looked strange and I felt confused, then from looking down I looked up.

"You weren't conscious of that". He pushed the coffee pot towards me and I felt thoroughly disconcerted, perplexed and disoriented. What was that?

"When I made contact with my mother," I said, "I felt I'd known her all my life."
"And your father?" "I had no problems with him."
"And what was the conclusion? And how do you relate now?"
I couldn't respond.
"Where did you get all this information?" he asked. "From a book that I've been reading about rejected children and their parents."
"A little knowledge is a dangerous thing."
"Do you read?"
"No, and who told you to do this?"
"The therapist."
"I thought so."
"You have got very lazy; why don't you do some Sociology, or did going to that Special School stop you?"

I said nothing. He made me feel very very guilty and ashamed of myself. Who was I to confront him? It became quite clear that he was not to be messed about; I'd never seen this side of him before. He was not properly fulfilling his role as priest; he was not properly fulfilling his role as social worker; he had allowed the initial shocking contact with my mother to take place without support, without advice, without counselling. Now he was manipulating me into blaming myself for my own state of mind. This episode had a long-lasting unconscious effect on me.

Just then the nun from the kitchen came in with another priest to see him.
"Come on, let Father have his dinner."
He offered me some more coffee.
"No thank you."
I left the dining room feeling totally confused and doubting myself; this doubt about the authenticity of my own experience was to become a recurrent theme. I was very angry.

I went back into therapy, but as the weeks went on things got no better. I constantly went over the past; the contact with my mother; her second rejection of me, a mental loop wishing I had never made the contact in the first place, blaming myself for not understanding her, feeling my energy completely drained by the whole process. Life seemed like a huge black hole which I could never climb out of. Fuck it.

In the end I rang Colehill again. "I don't think I'm able to get through this," I confessed. "We have a therapist at Colehill; Mrs Roy. I think that you won't get through it if you can't keep those feelings of anger at bay if they come up. You could get over your anger here."

Chapter Ten

Some time later I went down to Cardiff. I was determined to see my mother and get this thing sorted out. I went to her house and stood outside. I could hear my mother telling Paul to stop making that racket on his guitar, then she told him to get out. I stood there until he left, then knocked on the door. My father answered it, in his trousers and pullover (I never saw him wear a shirt). He said, "If you come on the scene now there will be arguments."

He took me off to a pub and bought me a pint, and himself an orange juice. We were sitting there, and I was getting a little drunk. I could hear him saying to himself: "He's just like his mother."
"That Father Tucker keeps on pestering me about all this," he said, "that fucking priest."
"You didn't have a good mother," I said, "is that right?" I was wondering if history was repeating itself. Having read some Jung, I was hoping I might free myself of the burden of the past.
"She used to hit me with the broom," he admitted. The conversation drifted away into early memories.
"As a child I never thought badly of you," I said.
"Maybe in two or three years she might try again," he wondered. And this would become a recurring theme.

Soon after that I came out of therapy with Hugh Millett, feeling mentally drained. I thought to myself, *'this therapist is only feeding back to me what I already know.'* I ripped up the notes that he had written about me in therapy, and then I felt guilty. But I thought *'I've made that decision, and I've got myself another place to live.'* I had found accommodation in a bed and breakfast place.

From a phone call to Coleshill, I learned that Paul Wright, my friend from nursery days, had gone into All Saints Hospital having attempted suicide. Then I learned that another old boy, Gerard Rossiter, had in fact succeeded; he had hanged himself from the clock tower in Chelmsley Wood. I arrived at Coleshill for his funeral. The service was held in the church in the grounds, the very church where I used to clean the floor as a little boy. There were several people there whom I knew. Gerard had grown up in the 'Cottage Homes', and several of the boys who had grown up with him were there, as well as others from St Edward's. He was buried in the local cemetery, in the grounds of the Anglican church. He was younger than me; an Afro-Caribbean about whom I knew little. Rumours circulated that he hated his mother.

After the funeral there was understandably a great deal of concern and anxiety in the air at the coffee party in the Cottage Home (now the Social Workers' offices). One suicide would be a tragedy; one suicide plus an attempt, plus a breakdown looked serious. Clearly some ex-residents were on the edge. Social workers seemed to be everywhere. Father Tucker had told one of them that I was homeless and needed some accommodation. He came over. I told him I was feeling very low. He asked if I needed any accommodation. I told him I didn't, and I was taken aback by this intrusion. "I don't even know you," I said. But nonetheless we managed to build up some rapport, the conversation continued and we went upstairs. I talked about my mother. "Do you want to see your records?" he asked.

"No, I know what this is all about," I said. I believed that having made contact with my mother, the only thing that really concerned me was whether this pattern of aggression and rejection was going to continue to act itself out through my own life as a repeating family history. This was the first time "records" were ever mentioned to me. At the time, I thought I really did know my own history, and so records had no significance for me at all.

"Do you think that you might do the same thing as your mother?" This was in fact what had been the problem all along, since that first contact with her when I was 17, but I wasn't going to admit that to a stranger. I gave no reply.

Downstairs I went and talked to Father Tucker:
"The past, present, and future are rolled into one. This ought to have been solved years ago," I said.
"I had my hands tied behind my back. You seem to have picked up all of the jargon." He sounded seriousy patronising.

Once again he succeeded in making me feel deeply uncomfortable about myself.

The Director, Mr Pinches, who was the first lay director of Father Hudson's, with a background in the Civil Service, spoke to us all. He was a tall thin man and sounded like a politician: "If you ever need our help please just ask;

Father Tucker is now the spiritual director of Father Hudson's." In my own situation, this didn't seem real. Was he saying that Father Hudson's was my 'family', and could be there for me? I went back home feeling very lonely.

I decided to go abroad again in order to shake off these unhappy associations and get myself back on track. I visited Paris for a while to see some friends. Meanwhile I was trying to recover from rebirth therapy and shake off some of the therapeutic jargon.

But after some weeks I took up the invitation and came back to Coleshill. I resented this as a backward step, feeling convinced that Father Tucker had caused the mess that I was in, but I was skint, I was unemployed, I was mentally unstable, and this was my only familiar point of reference. I went to speak to the new Assistant Director, responsible for the day-to-day renovations currently taking place. I asked him if he could find me any work on the 'farm', as a groundsman. I told him my story, but he had no suggestions as to how the institution might help me. "You're just running around like a headless chicken," he said.

Later in the grounds of Father Hudson's I met a Miss Joyce Carroll: a social worker whom I had previously encountered at Gerard's funeral. A middle-aged woman with a maternal manner, blondish curly hair and glasses, she spoke with a South Wales accent; this reminded me of my family and sounded very familiar and reassuring. This proved to be a dangerous misunderstanding; in fact she was able to build up an illusion of trust which was deceptive, and which for me personally was painfully destructive.

"You're a survivor" she told me. "You're too proud to ask for our help." She went on to talk about all the boys who are pushed out of children's homes too young to fend for themselves. "That's unnatural," she said, "no real family would do that". Father Tucker had told her that I was suicidal, and that it was my second rejection by my mother that had caused it. We continued our conversation in one of the old Cottage homes. By this time Father Hudson's homes and the nursery had completely closed; parts of the building in St Joan's were being renovated for disabled accommodation. It was a very different place and atmosphere from what I remembered; a disorienting experience.

"I have a bond with you," Joyce Carroll told me. "I can identify with you, I was in care myself." Then she told me her father had committed suicide. "There are parts of my past that I will never fully understand." She told me "in these contacts you need to hold on to the reins and pace things out a bit". She went on to say she knew of an old boy whose mother had not seen him since he was a baby, and he was very angry with her. This was a similar story to my own. Probably there are many more.

When I spoke to Joyce about my encounter with the Assistant Director, she just laughed, which I thought was heartless.

I talked to Sister Xavier, still working on the site of the hospital, which was now an old people's home. "Father Tucker didn't know how you were going take it. You can't judge them, love." I sat there crying, thinking even she didn't understand me, after all. She didn't understand what he had done; she still regarded the priest as being inevitably right in all circumstances.

Walking down the road I saw Father Tucker and said to one of the old boys I was walking with, "There's the man I hate." Father Tucker overheard.

A few days later I met him again. "People like you," said Tucker, "enjoy having power over other people. You are the cause of your mother's suffering. The records were fragmented. Your mother had a legal right to ring. You cannot force people to do things they don't want to do; you can't force your mother to accept you."
"Well, you can push them," I replied; "my therapeutic experience has taught me that".

"I thought the idea of therapy was to become responsible for your actions" responded Tucker, "but I don't know much about therapy. She might think of trying again. Maybe in two or three years you will be able to stand on your own two feet." This echoed remarks my father had made... Father Tucker went on to tell me that "She looked around for another nest for you". I pulled a face and made a near-silent grunt. He said "You have a chip on your shoulder. People like you have a design for revenge. I'm the sort of person who tells people what to do."

"Your mother said that she could not cope with you", he went on. "You had enough time to think about it here. I gave you a week to think about it". A week to think about *what,* I wondered? "To be a Christian is to do service, but you don't believe in that." I thought to myself *'well, who's the cause of my suffering?'* "Why are you back here?" he asked. I gave no reply.

I was talking to Joyce Carroll in the office some days later about what Father Tucker said to me. "That's a cop out," she said. "You should have been told earlier as you were growing up; then it would not have been so much of a shock. It shouldn't have been like Cilla Black's 'Surprise Surprise'; and where was the after-support? Who was supposed to pick up the pieces? "

"Can I have a look at my records?"
"No", she said, "we can't let you look at the records but we can give you a written history. You should write down your experience of being in Care." We went on to talk about mental hospitals. "Do you think I'm mad?" "No."

Then she told me about a woman who had gone into a mental hospital and then applied to emigrate, but because she was on the hospital computer records as having had treatment for mental illness, she couldn't. The thought of not been able to emigrate frightened me. I never wanted to go to a mental hospital. *In retrospect, I think this was a piece of psychiatric manipulation. It was intended to frighten me away from making contact with any medical professionals outside Father Hudson's, and it lodged in my mind very powerfully.*

I talked to Joyce Carroll about Father Tucker. "He has a very private life," she said. "You should be a psychiatrist for social workers," she went on. "But he's helped a lot of people spiritually."

She was playing two roles here. One role was to identify with me and my past. On the other hand she was trying to justify the way things had been handled, in an attempt to look after the interests of the church. These two roles were basically irreconcilable.

Feeling deeply frustrated about the whole situation I went to see Father Tucker again. He was in the office as I came in.

"You're the cause of my suffering," I said to him. I had been having appalling flashbacks, I told him. "Why didn't you talk to me?" he asked. I couldn't respond to this.

"You did not trust me", he went on. "If I had had more time I could have worked on your mother. What angered me is that she did not go through with it. These are delicate situations and require delicate handling. You fell down in the logic of it. And then there was all that time, and maybe she thought we had something on her." This was perplexing. What did he mean?

"She told me that she had post-natal depression," I said.
"Well there you go; diminished responsibility." Again I wondered what this meant?
"The law on this," he went on, "says that the initial contact can only be made by the adoptee."
"Have you ever prevented anyone from making contact?"
"Only once. I felt that he was a bit neurotic."

He moved his hand across the table.
"I was in the situation once, where when one breaks the relationship off and the other one is left wondering why."
Then he moved his hand back.
I said nothing. This was seriously confusing, did he mean that he had had a relationship? He was a priest.
All in all, this encounter made me feel even more depressed, and I said so.
"Then go to your doctor and get a tablet for the depression."

"When did my grandmother get in contact with you?" I asked.
"She contacted me a year after your mother had contacted me. I had written to her to say that you had had one disappointment and that you did not want another."
"I didn't think that much of her," I admitted. "I thought she was a bit neurotic and tried to put her off," he claimed.

But never, in this encounter or any other, did he suggest or admit that any part of my problems might have been his fault. It was my fault, or my mother's fault, but not the fault of the Church, or of the Society, or of any member of it.

I went over one evening to Father Tucker's house to talk: "Why do people do this work?" I asked. "Because it makes them feel good." *This seemed an odd reply for a priest to make, but for a social worker it would be acceptable. He too was trying to occupy two roles.*

"You know about psychology?" I asked. "Well, I did the life cycles," he replied. "What's that?" "It's about the life cycles of people."
"How would my mother feel?" "She would be feeling guilt."
"And my father?" "He would have wanted you both, but sometimes in situations like this the step-father doesn't know" (*stepfather? I thought? What?),* "and the mother has not said anything to him."

There had recently been a program on the television about a policeman who had his legs blown off by the IRA. Father Tucker made a comment about this and I had watched the same program myself. I pointed out that the police officer had no desire for revenge; he had dealt with his anger by firing at targets in the police station. *Nobody at Father Hudson's had offered me any way of dealing with mine.*

"It would have worked out," he claimed, but you had to play it your way. Some people never get over it. Therapy was the way you chose to rebuild your life; why didn't you give your rejection to God?"

This made me feel that I was a failure. I was hopelessly confused. What was 'his way'? He had said that 'two or three meetings will trigger off an acceptance', but they hadn't. I felt that he regarded my resorting to therapy as second best, and clearly he felt that I had rejected him. He was a qualified social worker; in fact the first priest from Father Hudson's ever to qualify as such. *But he was clearly unable to deal with the situation; he did not have the expertise to deal with my anger and feelings, and was covering his tracks.*

After we had stopped talking I thought, *'it was he that started talking about me facing the past in the first place, so what does he mean by talking about my choice in rebuilding my life?* ' Tucker seemed a man full of contradictions, and indeed he was, as later revelations were to show.

67

Soon afterwards I had to move. I was put in the situation where I either had to leave the Home and get a place for myself or move up to Stoke, so I went to see Mr. Pinches.

We talked. "Why do I have to move?"
"Well, too many cooks spoil the broth." I had been talking to Joyce Carroll, having therapeutic sessions with Geraldine Roy, talking to Father Tucker, talking to the assistant director.... I could see what Mr Pinches meant. So with the help of yet another social worker, I moved to Stoke-on-Trent.

Chapter Eleven

Soon after that I left for Stoke on Trent, but I hated it. It was a Father Hudson's property, but I found that it was actually an institution for ex-offenders. What was that about? I couldn't understand why I should have been sent there. I was there for about six weeks. The therapist Mrs. Roy had been told by Mr Pinches the Director that I was not to go back to Coleshill, so I left and went down to Cardiff to see what it would be like to live there. It was 1986.

I went to Llandaff where my mother lived and visited a pub there, hoping to meet one of the members of my family. I got myself a drink and sat down. Some people came in and looked at me, and then one said, "Hello Sean." "I'm not Sean." "Who are you?" "Karl." "Karl who?" "Bicknell." "Never heard of you."

They came over and sat down and talked to me.
"I'm sorry to hear about your brother Stefan." "Why?" "Didn't you know? He's dead. It was in the South Wales Echo. I thought you would have known. I'm sorry for telling you." I told them my story.
"I can't understand a mother that would do that."
After finishing my drink, feeling very shocked, I stood outside the pub and thought *'my mother did not deserve that'.*

On the Sunday I went over to my mother's house with some flowers and put them on the doorstep. Seeing a shadow at the door Paul came, and I ran away. He came running after me; "Don't you want to see us?"

I stopped and look around. There was my mother following behind with the card that I had put with the flowers. She was looking me in the eyes, and I looked into hers.

"Do I look concerned about you?" she asked. "I feel sorry for you, but *I* haven't got a mother. If I could do something for you now I would. You've messed up my life since I was twenty one. I was out the back just now and I was going to commit suicide. I don't have anything left."   Moving from side to side she started to cry. She turned to Paul and put her arms around him.
"This is all I've got left."
I put my hand on her.

"You have" - she pulled away – "you have put a curse on the family."
She walked up the street, and I was left looking after her as she went.

"What was all that about?" asked Paul.
"She had post-natal depression after having me," I replied, "and as a result of that she put me into care."

"So how did Stephan die?" I asked. "She came home and dad was asleep and she found him." "He was nice." "Yes."

Later I read the Echo and found that he had died by accident from auto-asphyxiation, in a wardrobe, during sexual experimentation...

We talked a little more and he said he would come and meet me for a drink. Then one day later, walking into town, thinking and listening to Pat Metheny music on my Walkman I sat down on a bench. I could not believe Stephan was dead. 'She'll never get over that,' I thought, 'that door is closed in my face now.' My mind flashed back as if time had stood still. He was the one I had asked "Did you know you had another brother?" that morning, going over to Coleshill. The first brother I met.

"Remember me," I'd said to him. The words came back and I remembered a time when I was little, telling my mother "he's crying." I listened to the music; each chord went straight though me. I started crying, feeling warm at the same time.

After so much crying I got a headache. The music played on. Then looking up at the town, seeing people go past, unable to stop myself I started crying again. I was going through my memories again as the music played on in my ears from my Walkman.

I had met someone from the Art College, so I went along and did a bit of art work to get away from the language therapy. One day, sitting in a performance art workshop, I was watching what seemed like a play. Not knowing what to expect, it reminded me of therapy. The audience was part of the performance. There was a discussion afterwards. Somebody said, "You must have wanted this; you must have wanted to come to the workshop." This made connections for me; how much had I wanted to make contact with my family?

I sat there thinking of what Father Tucker had said, 'the time to ring your mother is at seven o' clock, but *only if you want to.*' All the time knowing the other members of the family did not know about me.

Hugh had said 'do the rebirth therapy, *but only if you want to.*' Father Tucker had said 'two or three meetings will trigger off an acceptance.'
Hugh had said 'two or three meetings will trigger off an acceptance.' Had they both read the same textbook on therapy?

Going through the whole thing in my mind, as if I was looking at performance art from the outside, I went over the contact that I had had with my mother and the interview that I had had with Father Tucker in his office. He said that he had lost contact with her and that I came into care at eighteen months. That meant that the only way contact could have been made would have been by my mother ringing. The fact that he had the records on his lap made it easier for me to believe that he was telling the truth, and that made it easier for him to push me into contact with her, because he knew that at the time I asked I *would* want to get in contact with her.

Father Tucker had put me in a trap all those years ago. I thought that even if he had given me a week as he'd said I had nothing to think about other than what he had told me. Then I thought it was possible for him to have known that I was rejected and that's why he'd said this was the root of the rejection, but then he had denied knowing about it in the priest's dining room. That's why he had me kicked out of the Murters', because he wanted me back in Coleshill so that I would undergo therapy with *him*. But things didn't work out like that for him.

Over the next months Paul did not contact me or come out for a drink. Feeling so frustrated with what my mother had said to me about Steven's death I thought *'I'm not having this'*, so after having a drink I rang her up.
"Hello", she said in her soft voice. "You child-batterer," I responded, "you've messed up my life since I was seventeen."
Then I slammed the 'phone down, and felt very guilty about what I'd said.

I spent about six months in Cardiff, resolving nothing.

Eventually I came back to Malvern. I was still feeling very unhappy with everything and not getting on with people in the house in which I was living. A friend recommended I go to see a homoeopath and, not feeling too sure about whether or not this would work, I rang Joyce Carroll up: "I feel suicidal." "I'm not having this, I think you need to see a psychiatrist." I flashed back to what she had said in the office and thought *a psychiatrist is the last person that I want to see*. That triggered off all the anxiety she had engendered long ago with a story about a woman who went to see a psychiatrist and as a result couldn't emigrate. I felt frightened of the possibility. But maybe my mother was right? Maybe this *was* all my fault?

Joyce said that she would ring the following day, and she did.
"I just rang to see how you were."
"I didn't say that I was going to commit suicide, I said that I felt suicidal."
We talked a little more and then said goodbye.

I decided to take up the recommendation to a homeopath and went to see Jeremy Sherr. He was a South African Jew who later became extremely distinguished and proved several new homeopathic remedies. Homeopathy is based on the principle of 'like curing like', and on the principle that the smaller the dose, the more powerful. He listened to my story, and gave me a remedy. This had a huge effect. My energy levels rose, and it was very refreshing not to be deluged with therapeutic jargon.

Later I went back to see Geraldine Roy. I told her that I had a homoeopathic remedy. Her attitude was that therapy and homeopathy could certainly work together, provided I was totally honest about my thoughts, feelings and dreams. She was a Freudian analyst. Her fees must have been paid by Father Hudson's; several ex-residents and clients who came to Father Hudson's for one reason or another were referred to her, and were all presumably paid for by the society. Freudian analysis is notoriously very expensive. So Hudson's at last was taking some moral responsibility for my mental breakdown?
But all Geraldine Roy was doing was putting me into the same trap that Father Tucker had over the contact with my mother by saying: "Didn't you want to know there was someone out there for you?" and then "You must have wanted to make contact." Did this mean the whole situation was my fault?

I told her what my mother had said to me after my brother's death. "She has made up her mind," said Mrs Roy. *How do you know?* I wondered. And then she said, "You're acting it out." This meant that in Freudian terms I was not really trying to resolve my problems; I was simply acting them out all over again by going to Cardiff.

I began to feel that she was treating me as a schizophrenic. Once again, as with so many therapists, her language was heavily jargon-ridden. And because these therapeutic encounters are confidential, and conducted behind closed doors, no public blame could ever be attached to anyone – except to me, myself.

I had nowhere settled to live; I had been evicted from the place where I was living in Malvern because I smashed a window during an argument with my landlady, who had a tendency to come into my room without asking.

I went up to Father Hudson's to see about some accommodation, and saw Mrs. Bellamy the new Assistant Director. I told her I was chronically depressed. She was a psychiatric social worker with an enormous bosom and an upper middle class accent. "You don't seem depressed to me," she said. I realized at once that she was not going to help me psychologically, but I still tried to explain my situation to her. "I just need a place to sort my life out."

"You mean a place of safety? So you need to be broken down and need some one to catch you, you need some support? If you didn't have a breakdown at St. Vincent's, it still might happen anywhere; it might happen on the bus one day. You've probably had too much therapy. I think maybe you are playing at therapy."
"How do you know?" I asked. "Because I worked in a psychiatric hospital for ten years. Are you some sort of hippy left over from the sixties?"
I gave no reply.

I rang Joyce Carroll up some days later. "You were interviewing her when she was interviewing you," she said. She laughed. So was my life simply a game to be played with?

On the other hand, the homoeopathic remedies that I had taken over the months were working. They were far more successful than any talking therapy. I felt much better integrated and balanced; some of my youthful confidence had returned and I had a spring in my step.

Empowered by this returning confidence, I rang Miss Carroll and said "I don't want to do any more therapy with Mrs. Roy," "You don't trust her," said Joyce Carroll. "You won't let anybody get close to you." It was true that I didn't trust her; I didn't whole-heartedly trust Joyce Carroll. They were both employed by the Society which had caused so much damage to my health and well-being. Was it true that I didn't trust *anybody*? I had certainly trusted people before the contact with my mother; could I not do so again? I had trusted friends in France; I was beginning to trust Jeremy Sherr. But many talking therapies have a tendency to put the client into a box which fits the therapeutic theory. If they can't do that they make a special box for you to fit.

"I've just had a homoeopathic remedy," I told her. "It's connected things back up and I feel better." "That's a delusion, just stick with Geraldine Roy."
She made me feel completely mad. Feeling better was a delusion?

Presently I made contact with another homoeopath, Dr Willie Monteiro, and I learned that he was a qualified psychiatrist. A tall handsome black guy, he introduced me to the ideas of Neuro-Linguistic Programming (NLP). At much the same time I went to visit a friend in Oxford, and in Blackwell's bookshop found a book on James Tyler Kent, a copy of the Organon of Samuel Hahnemann, and 'Uncommon Therapy' by Milton K. Ericson. So I began to read about therapy, about homeopathy, and got to grips with Ericson's theories of structured hypnosis, and how he used language and body-language in a very artful and skilful way to help his clients. He also used strategies which were effectively interventions in their lives order to make changes, thus blocking out choice. In retrospect this is morally questionable and very highly manipulative; but it was a very powerful influence on NLP.

My reading led me to realize that much of Father Tucker's 'work' with me had been informed by these ideas. Ericson talks about 'life cycles' and that triggered a memory. Father Tucker had said "I've done the life cycles". Was this the book that he had read? Dr Will told me, "People who have therapy confront a higher set of problems than they had in the beginning. They have to return to their original vulnerable state without any fresh resources." He equipped me with valuable new skills to deal with life's ups and downs, and linguistic skills that were helpful in coping with other people, and indeed even with writing. This whole process gave me the confidence to begin to challenge the institution which had caused me such harm.

Chapter Twelve

From all that I had learned over the years I could not get out of my head what Father Tucker had told me in Care in that interview; that I was eighteen months old when I went to Father Hudson's, but my mother said 'four and a half'.

At that time, legislation was pushed through to give care leavers access to their records. (This access was to be at the discretion of the local authorities and the health authorities. However, I went to the Citizen's Advice Bureau and found that this legislation did not extend to private organisations such as Father Hudson's.)

I rang Miss Carroll repeatedly over several months, asking for the case notes which she had promised so long ago.
"You know you said that you would give me a copy of my case history; would you do that for me?"
She repeatedly refused, or prevaricated. Once at Christmas she offered 'a pullover which I've got here for you', but a few weeks later she had forgotten all about it.

Then *she* accused *me* of being manipulative.
Adamant that I was not going to accept this, I asked again, "Would you write the case history out for me please?" and I put the 'phone down.

During one of our many frustrating conversations I said that I had "just been reading the D.H.S.S. thing that just came out." And she admitted "I read that in September."

"What did Father Tucker say to you ?"
"He said that I came into Care at eighteen months old, and he said that the records were fragmented."
"Oh, we didn't take very good notes in those days."
"Would you write the case history out?"
"I think you didn't accept that you were in Care." What did she mean by this? What sort of denial was I supposed to be in? If I hadn't accepted that I was in care, why would I be making any of these investigations?
"Well, if you write that I came into Care at eighteen months I will send it back to you to write again." She continued to use delaying tactics.

I rang again:
"Did you get my letter?"
"I'm very pleased that you wrote to us."

I thought 'the patronising bitch.' Thinking of the school I went to.

"I've been reading a book on N.L.P. Do you do N.L.P. on your clients?"
"That's what you are doing to yourself."
"Are you going to write the case history?"
"Are you trying to blame society? It was your parents."
"No one is blaming anybody," I insisted. "I would just like you to write up the case history as you said you would. Thank you."

Coming off the 'phone I was thinking *'this woman's trying to re-paint my reality. All this is just standard social policy.'* I thought of getting some spray paint and writing on the wall of the Home 'Stop mental illness - kill a social worker.' Then I thought that if Miss Carroll had her way she would have me in a mental hospital. They love the incapable and they want to keep you that way. I wrote on paper at home 'little boxes, little boxes, we're all in little boxes.' I thought of sending it off, but didn't.

I rang Miss Carroll again but she was out and Mrs. Howard the receptionist answered it: "Miss Carroll said to tell you we have told you everything that you need to know."

So it was clear that I was not going to get any further by negotiation. I began to realize that only legal action would help. The organization which had looked after me as a child was now betraying me; denying me my own history. Until now, I had to a great extent blamed myself for failing to establish a good connection with my family. Naturally I had a strong sentimental attachment to Father Hudson's, but now I began to reject some of those feelings. I began to see that maybe the whole affair had been managed very badly by Father Tucker. How could he have allowed me to contact my mother so suddenly, at 17, without any kind of preparation, or history, or support? I needed help to deal with multiple layers of emotional attachment and separation; attachment to Father Hudson's and the nuns, to Father Tucker himself, to my parents. And I was offered none. In this situation I found that I became detached and clinical in my views. This was to be my survival technique, and it continues to this day. So I went to a solicitor, explained my story to him and he sent a letter off to Mr Pinches, the principal.

I heard nothing, so after some weeks I rang Mr. Pinches myself: "What are you going to do about my solicitor's letter?"
I was thinking *'they can't do much about it; they will have to let me look at the records now.'*
"I've given it to Mrs. Bellamy."
At last, weeks later, the reply came back.
"As a private organisation we do not hand over our records."

I felt so mad I wanted to burn the place down, but if I did that I would go to prison. Or break in and get the records that way, but then they would know ....

I called up Mrs. Bellamy on the 'phone: "You have no right to do this," I said, "these records are not yours." "I can understand that you would want something belonging to your mother," she replied, "but we cannot hand over the records to you. What is your motive for asking?" Was this a bluff?

"My motive is to make sure that you do not do this to another person", I replied, "and to put the appropriate ball into the appropriate court. What my mother is responsible for she is responsible for, and what you're responsible for you're responsible for."

However fragmented my records were, if they were fragmented at all, even if several pieces of the full story were missing, it was impossible that Father Tucker had not known that I was abused as a child before I joined Father Hudson's. If he truly did not know the full circumstances, he certainly had a remarkable insight into a situation that he did not officially know anything about. He had pushed me into contact with my mother, while telling me "only if I wanted to". I now understood that, having learned some psychotherapy, he had done this in order to throw my unconscious into my conscious mind so that I would break down and break apart, so that he could find the root of the rejection, creating a mental loop between what she said and what he said. The conflict between his "eighteen months" and her "four and a half years" had been engineered by him to achieve this kind of breakdown. Now that I had studied so much psychotherapy myself, I could understand what he had tried to do. He had asked "don't you want to resolve the past? Anger distorts the personality." But meanwhile he had denied me my past, by refusing to allow me access to my records. These were seriously conflicted messages. Of course anger was distorting my personality. This remark remained imprinted on my mind for many years, as though with indelible ink.

"And you're demented about it," said Barbara Bellamy, in his defence. "Maybe it was so awful that he could not tell you? What did Father Tucker say?" If my childhood was so awful that no-one could tell me about it, I thought, why did Father Tucker ever put me back in touch with my mother at all?
"He said that I came into Care at eighteen months old. Was he drunk when he was reading the records?"
"And what is mummy saying to you?"

'I've played that game before in therapy' I thought to myself. *'This is about parent/adult/child transactional analysis.'* These exchanges were multi-layered; part official jargon, part psychotherapeutic jargon, part legal jargon, part religious jargon, and very frustrating to cope with. Simplicity had gone out of the window.

"She said I was four and a half; my sister remembered that, and my grandmother too. Father Tucker said the records were fragmented; concerning a situation that he did not know anything about officially." "Why would we lie to you?" There was a pause.

"So then are you calling my mother a liar?" I asked in return. "Father Tucker said that I was illegitimate, and now I know that I have brothers and a sister, and I look just like them." "So why would we lie?"
"To keep his integrity intact," I replied.

"O. K., then I will have to arrange a case conference. So what is the best date for you to come up?"
We made a date.

Chapter Thirteen

Presently a date was set for a meeting. I came up to Coleshill and went straight to the Social Worker's office in the old cottage homes, and there I saw Miss Carroll.

"You have to go over to the other side," she said, "to the main office." I walked into the main office carrying my book of James Tyler Kent on Homeopathic Philosophy. One of the secretaries asked "Are you running the country?"

I gave no reply, and walked into the main office, to find Mrs Howard the receptionist, and Barbara Bellamy, now the assistant director (the position formerly held by Father Tucker before he became spiritual director).
"Mrs Howard would you make a cup of tea for us both?"
"Certainly."

We then walked into Father Tucker's old office and both sat down. She sat behind a large imposing desk; I was seated to one side. The whole experience was intimidating to say the least. There was an awkward pause.
"So what do you do for a job?" she asked.
"I work in a pizza parlour."
"Oh! I like the pepperoni ones," she said, trying to build rapport.

As she talked she moved from side to side on her swinging chair, making me feel even more uneasy, and then wrote what I did for work on a piece of paper. The whole scene was deeply patronising. And the room was full of powerful memories, both good and terrifying. It was this office that my father had come to the first time I saw him; it was in this room that I had had many pleasant and reassuring conversations with Father Tucker; and it was from this room that I had made the second telephone call to my mother. Presently Mrs. Howard came in with the tea and then left. After a few sips and some small talk, Barbara Bellamy turned to the matter in hand.

Still swinging confidently in her chair, she said "Your mother felt that she was endangering you as a child, do you consider yourself to be endangered now?"
"No!"
"Do you feel persecuted?"

"No!" I declared, thinking *she thinks I'm a schizophrenic.*
"....Oh! On the file there was a school report which said that you had stabbed a boy with a pair of scissors, that there was blood everywhere and the mother of the child had written to the Home, do you remember that?"
I thought hard...
"No." I certainly did not have any recollection of stabbing anybody with a pair of scissors. All I remembered was being so unhappy.
"....Do you have a desire to kill your mother with a knife?"
"No!"

"....most people like you do", she responded. *Was she all-knowing? What did she mean 'people like me?' Which psychiatric group did I fall into?*
"That's your opinion," I replied. "From a homeopathic point of view the person with the knife has a desire to come together with the person stabbed. I know a homeopath, Jeremy, who has taught me a lot about homoeopathic philosophy, he's a bit like a god to me."
"Fascinating; I did a PhD. in philosophy."
"It's a useless subject unless you can use it," I said.
"Yes... oh like a god you said, you only see one in relationships, not twos and threes?" *She was clearly trying to identify me as a schizophrenic who had never left the stage of total identity with his mother, let alone reached an adult stage of socialization.*

"What do you mean?" I asked.
"You only see one person in relationships, not the twos and threes. It's all or nothing for you. Your mother had wanted you adopted and a nun went up to see her. When the nun walked in to see your mother she was very confused to see a smiling boy bouncing on his mother's knee and that they both seemed quite happy. It was not until your mother had kept on running around to her parish priest that you came into Care."

I smiled at the thought of me on my mother's knee.
"Did my mother have postnatal depression?"
"There's no record of it, but there is a note from a psychiatrist on record. Your father came up to see you once at Father Hudson's but you didn't recognise him."
"Yes I did! I came running down the cloister and there he was and I remember thinking *'oh it's you.'*"

"Your mother wanted you in a home in Cardiff but father said no". This was very confusing, but I couldn't ask for explanation, I was emotionally paralysed. *Which father? My own father? Father Coyne? Father Flint?*
"Father said that you would be happy in the Children's Home. There's a note on file to say that you were happy with the nuns."
"I knew the nun who looked after me loved me, because one night after I had done something wrong she cried."
"Do you consider love to be hurtful to people?"
What an extraordinary question. "No."
"What do you think love is?"
I said nothing.
"You can't love in a socially acceptable way." *Is this what one responsible adult should be saying to another?*
I referred to my homeopathic philosophy. "The only thing that's real is nature, because nature just loves, and it's our capacity to pick it up."

She looked out of the window and then turned back to face me. Her upper-middle-class authoritarian voice replied. "Your mother regularly sent your Family Allowance except when your father was out of work; she was very good about this; these days we take it from the parents at source. Your mother applied to go to Africa and wanted you adopted, and Father thought that it was a good idea."

I thought to myself '*who said that? because at the time my case was being handled by Canon Flint.*' "But your father refused."
I just smiled.
"Your mother divorced your father in 1974."
"That was because of his drinking, my mother said."
"Well, coming up from the mine he would be thirsty…. your parents were playing bat and ball with you." *How did she know? How patronising could she be?*

I decided to move out of this minefield into a different area and assert some kind of autonomy. "And my grandmother?" I asked.
"Your grandmother had written to the Catholic Children's Society. Your mother said she'd had some problems with her mother." *She did not elaborate on this; what did she mean?*

I looked at a photograph of hers by the desk.
"Is that Italy or France?" I asked; the photo showed children standing in front of a building with a notice saying *Assistant Social.*
"Fascinating, have you ever done an I.Q. test?"
"No; why?"
"You speak very well." I thought to myself, *'this is very stupid, considering the fact that I can mimic almost anybody'.* This was becoming a battle of wits.
"And what's an IQ test?"
"It's just putting things together. When you came into Care you didn't speak; the Special School must have helped you out there."
"Why did you ask about the IQ test?"
"Because you asked if the photograph was of Italy or France. It's France." There was another pause. "When you came into Care you had bruise marks on your back and your mother said that she'd done this."
"Father Tucker told me he knew nothing about any abuse. In fact he said that I was the cause of my mother's suffering." Barbara seemed quite surprised by this. She leant forward in her chair.
"He knew that he couldn't be attacked when he said that," I said. *He put me in an emotional straitjacket*, I thought.

"In a hospital where I worked", she responded, "I once went to see the psychiatrist about one of the patients I felt that he was wrong about. I remember sitting on this very uncomfortable chair, talking about this patient and feeling so frustrated with the psychiatrist and being unable to move from this chair. I went back through this in a psychodrama, I remembered this chair." She laughed.
"And being so frustrated I was able to work this out in the drama because I felt angry with the psychiatrist."
Was this supposed to establish that she felt some identification with me? Did she think I could resolve my history through some simple psychodrama? And live happily ever after?

"There's a note on file saying there was a fire in your work place, and the staff at St. Vincent's were quite concerned about you." *What on earth was this about? what did the records say?* "Yes", I said, "I couldn't get to work fast enough that day." I remembered the excitement of seeing smoke billowing out of the warehouse near the Post Office tower. *Her remark was intended to trigger my memory of the crucial phone call which set my troubles in motion. It succeeded.*

"Yes, Father Tucker rang me at St. Vincent's; he told me my mother had rung that day and, only if I wanted to, I could ring her at 7 o' clock. When I rang all the past came up. I felt psychologically raped. I went round to see him some weeks later, he said that was the root of the rejection, and that two or three meetings would trigger off an acceptance."
"Oh," she said, leaning forward again, "the American style of face-to-face confrontation, and you were flooded out. Fascinating." *How could she trivialize as 'fascinating' something so horribly painful and difficult?*

I began to try to explain what this encounter had done to me. "I felt very guilty," I said "about whether I would treat a woman in the same way that my mother had treated me. I went through mental torture for a long time over that one, I felt sexually perverted; I had a complete breakdown."
"Can you prove you had a breakdown?" *This flipped me back to my conversation with Joyce Carroll about the woman and the psychiatrist.* I couldn't reply. I gazed around the room and my eye fell on a picture of Mary.

Barbara saw what I was looking at. "Did you have any delusions about your mother?" she asked. *So now I was supposed to be delusional as well?*
I talked about my experience of Neuro-Linguistic- Programming with Dr Willie Monteiro. At this point her ears pricked up and she showed keen interest. "He'll be in the Directory of Psychiatrists!" she said. "I went to see him privately," I pointed out, so she realized there wouldn't be any NHS records of my breakdown or treatment.
I began to talk about The NLP techniques of disassociating myself from painful memories by looking at myself from outside. "Oh, the out-of-body experience" she said in a patronizing tone, "How fascinating!"

She steered back to my childhood history. "Were you sexually abused?" "No," I said.
"You weren't *put* into care at eighteen months" she told me. "You were *referred* to care then." She then handed me two photo-stat copies of my admission to Father Hudson's when I was three years and ten months. "Father Tucker didn't lie," she affirmed. "His integrity is completely intact." This implied that it was my parents' integrity and indeed my own, that was in question.

Finally she handed me a leaflet about psychodrama sessions. At last I had got some answers, and I began to cry. She came across from behind her desk and put her arms around me.
"Can I keep in touch with you?" I asked. She moved back and flinched.
"I'm leaving soon," she replied
"Oh, what are you going to do?"
"I'm going to work with sexually abused children."
"I thought you would."
The 'phone rang, and I went to see Mr. Pinches next door in his office.
"Thank you for that."
"Well, I'm pleased that we were able to help you. If ever we can help in the future we will."
I shook hands and said goodbye, then asked the receptionist to say goodbye to Mrs. Bellamy for me.

I got back to Worcester very late, thinking in my confusion *'how the fuck would my father know whether I was happy in the Children's Home?'* I felt as if I had been a prisoner there. *I've spent fourteen years in that Home, I thought, and he didn't even want the other members of the family to know I existed.*

The following day I looked at the leaflet I'd been given. *'All I'll be doing with this is what I already know',* I thought and put the leaflet back into my drawer. *'I'm not going through that again.'* I saw myself like some schizophrenic going through psychodrama and killing my mother with a knife. Then I started to think hard about what she had said about my being eighteen months old, that seemed puzzling.

I thought of writing back to the Home and asking for some proof of this, but I didn't. I thought to myself *'that woman thinks I'm a dangerous psychopath; I think she fancied herself as a psychiatrist.'* If I had spent three years with Mrs. Roy I would have been patting her on the back by now, saying "thank you for helping me with my problem", when they had created it in the first place. I went out and sat in a coffee shop thinking over all that had happened in the past with my mother. I started to cry, feeling so guilty about the way that I had behaved to her, but then I thought *'it wasn't my fault, if I had known what was going on things would have been different.'*

Then I rang Mrs. Bellamy: "Were you doing an assessment of me?"
"No," she laughed.
"What my mother did she could not help, but what you did you could help, and you have caused a lot of damage with what you did."
Then I put the 'phone down.

I went to see Dr Willie and spoke to him about the interview that I had just had. I was thinking *'I would love to smash Father Tucker's kneecaps'*, when he said "You should have asked her why things didn't work out if Father Tucker was so right." Then we did some N.L.P.

I rang Father Tucker.
"Why did you say that I was put into Care at eighteen months when I came into Care at four and a half? Why did you say the records were fragmented? Why did you have me kicked out of the Murter house? Why did you deny that I had been abused? Why did you say that you had lost contact with my mother when she was actually sending you the Family Allowance? Why did you say at the funeral of one of the old boys that you had your hands tied behind your back? Why did you say that I was illegitimate?"
"You have asked me about fifteen questions."
"I suppose you are going to justify yourself under some perverted psychology?"
"Have you said everything?"
"Yes."
"So have I. Thank you, goodbye."
And he put the 'phone down.

I thought after that I was going totally mad.

Chapter Fourteen

When I got back to see Mrs. Bellamy I asked whether they were going to pay Doctor William. "Yes." I told her what I had said to Father Tucker on the 'phone. "That's called deflection, he's pushing it back to you."

Over the months that passed I would go over in my mind the interviews that I'd had, and the things that had happened. I was very confused; was I in fact some kind of psychopathic personality type? Or not? Maybe the Children's Home was right? If I'd been abused, was I really likely to abuse? I became obsessional, with an aversion to knives, in case I really subconsciously did want to kill my mother. I thought of writing to her but then, every time I thought about it, it would just depress me. I hated that Children's Home and what it had done to me.

I went on working with Willie Monteiro. We did an exercise whereby he took me in my mind back into the priest's dining room, where Father Tucker was making all those apparently involuntary twitches. Willie used neuro-linguistic-programming techniques to allow me to observe the whole scene from outside. This disassociation was very liberating. Willie pointed out that Father Tucker had been abusing his position, and indeed abusing me, in the context of my history. Ericson wrote about the use of twitches and bodily movements as well as contradictory language to induce a trance-like state.

This was only one of many techniques that Willie used to dislodge my mind from its poor state. He enabled me to change my perception of depression, and this alone was very helpful. He would say things like, " I used to listen to classical music, because it gave my depression meaning. Some of the most creative people are depressive." This was very far from the conventional stuff I'd been fed up till now. I began to read more about NLP. Gradually I have come to know that in the wrong hands it can be a dangerous weapon; it is a manipulative technique and should be handled with some caution. I was lucky to find Willie, but of course I had been deeply unlucky with Father Tucker. Eventually Willie told me that he had written to the Home saying that there was some improvement in my state, and that he would not charge the full amount. I was quite angry about this, considering the damage they had caused me.

But I certainly was much better. I enrolled to do a course in carpentry, and found myself a job with Hereford and Worcester County Council on a government training scheme; ('an extra tenner' it was called).

One Saturday, I came downstairs from my flat in Worcester to find a letter on the mat. I opened it up. It was from the D.H.S.S saying "we do not take responsibility for the contents of the enclosed letter." The 'enclosed letter' was from the Salvation Army talking about a missing person, and saying "we believe that you are the person that we are looking for. If you are not the person that we are looking for would you please contact us and cite the reference number 186/ 4556."

A telephone number and address were included, and there was a note which read :

The Salvation Army Social Services Investigation Department
Enquiry reference number - 189/4556
Person making the enquiry - Kathleen Maddison Wheeler
Date of birth - 2. 11. 1919
Person sought - Karl Bicknell
Date of birth- 13. 01. 1962
Last known address – unknown, in Birmingham
Relationship to enquirer - grandson
Other information - your grandmother asks that we inform you that she is much better now than the last time you saw her.

At first I felt quite confused thinking 'who is this person Kathleen Wheeler?' then eventually realizing, 'oh, yes, it *is* my grandmother.' She was married to a man called Mr. Wheeler. I tucked the note into my pocket and went and had a coffee in the shop wondering whether or not to reply. I kept the letter in the flat and sat there looking at it accusingly. I thought over everything I had said to my mother after my brother's death, and what my grandmother had said to me in her house at Stratford. She had told me that when she died she would leave me everything. I had a very strong feeling that she was dying. I thought of what Barbara Bellamy, Joyce Carrol and Father Tucker had said to me in the past, and of what I now knew; that that priest was lying.

From the conflict inside myself I thought of sending the letter to my mother asking, "Is this a joke? I think this belongs to you", as she had told me that she did not have a mother. Then I thought *'she has found me, and I have a strong feeling she is going to die soon.'* It was all deeply unsettling to say the least. But at the same time this contact was really necessary. I went to see a friend and told him about the letter. He said,

"If you love you grandmother, you will contact her, you can only say yes or no." It was that 'yes or no' that I did not like to think about. I did not want to fall into the same trap as I had all those years ago with my mother; was this going to end up with yet another rejection? Or was this some kind of family game in which I was a pawn? Each day at work I went over and over it in my mind. I told some other friends, making a joke about it - perhaps I should just go and visit her in a black suit next week, to be ready for the event.

Anyway, I felt that I had made a choice no. Looking back, I decided that I had had enough problems with social workers, that I never wanted them to be involved in my life again. I decided that I would see her once and that would be it. I sent her a letter asking her how she was. I asked how my brother and sister were getting on and told her that I worked in Hereford and Worcester and that I was at college at the moment. Some weeks later a letter came back, in very untidy handwriting.

Monday March 5th 1990   Mr L.S. Wheeler
                             119 Chapel Wood
                             Llanedeyrn
                             Cardiff
                             South Glamorgan
                             South Wales CF3 7EG

Dear Karl,
I have just had a letter from the Salvation Army with the wonderful news that they have found you. I am your grandmother's husband (Larry). I am writing this on her behalf as she is in hospital, she been there for over 2 weeks with a severe stroke. I visit her every day and her condition is slightly better, she can hear you and see you but of course can't speak. They can do such wonderful things now and all we can do is hope. I have seen her today and she looked a little better especially when I told her you had been found. Her eyes lit up, so I know she understood. Your uncle Steven always asks if we have heard how and where you are. I will phone and tell him the good news tonight. Of course it's a long way for you to travel down here.
--- will give you my phone number. If you can phone it's Cardiff --0222 –7xxxxx, I am out all day so evening time would be the best and the cheapest. uncle--- crossed out---
Steven's number 0222 5xxxxx. Again evenings as he is working all day. Please contact me by phone or letter Karl, it must be about ten years since we saw you. Looking forward to hearing from you when you can. All the very best to you, and I hope you do well at college.
Best wishes to you from myself and on behalf of your grandmother Kathy,

Yours sincerely,

Mr. L S. Wheeler.

After reading the letter, I sat in the flat and felt very guilty that I had not kept in contact with her. Finally I rang up Steven. "Hello."
"It's Karl."
"We were expecting a call from you; I'm Elizabeth, Steven's at work at the moment; where are you living, London?"
"No, Worcester."
"Where to?" (in her Cardiffian accent).
I laughed. "Where to? Worcester."
"You sound just like your brothers." ('No, I thought, really?')
"So what happened to my grandmother?"
"We were at a family party and your grandmother looked as if she had fallen asleep on the table, it could have happened at any time. Well she had a good life."

We went on to talk about my family and about her family. "We were on holiday with your mother, she wouldn't talk about you." Then Steven came in and Elizabeth said that I was on the 'phone, so he picked it up.
"Hello mate."
"I don't know what to say to you now."
"You speak very posh," he said.
We talked for some time about the family and what I was doing, and I gave him my address and work 'phone number, then he said "I'd like to meet you, we could go out for a drink, have you rung up Larry?"
"No, not yet."

We said our goodbyes then I rang up Larry.
"Hello."
"It's Karl."
"Oh, hello kid."
We talked about my grandmother for some time.
"Can I come down to see her?"
"Your mother comes over to collect me to take me to the hospital and I don't want any animosity between the two of you in front of your grandmother, so just send her a card. Have you rung Steven?"
"Yes, so I will send her a card then."

"Yes, she'll like that."

Some days later, I rang up Steven and asked how my grandmother was.
"Still very much the same."
"I'm sorry for ringing."
"That's O.K"
I spoke to him about the Children's Home. I knew they were lying to me.
"I've got a chip on my shoulder myself about some of the things that happened," he said. "We all want to meet you, Vic and Val and Maria. You could stay here and then we can go and see her in the hospital tomorrow.
"God, that's very soon."
We spoke a little more, then said goodbye.

Over the next week, I thought about the meeting. It would resolve some of their guilty feelings for not contacting my grandmother over the years. I thought of asking Coleshill whether my grandmother had contacted them so I rang them.

I was shaking on the 'phone speaking to Miss Carroll :
"Did my grandmother get in contact with you?"
"No", she said quickly.
"You lied to me in the past by saying that I was put into Care at eighteen months old."
"Four and half", she said very quickly.
"So why wouldn't you lie to me again."
I put the 'phone down.

Some days later, a message from Steven arrived at work saying the weekend might be cancelled. So I rang up.
"Is the weekend cancelled?"
"No, I'll get back in touch with you."

I thought my grandmother must have died or something must have happened to Steven's children. Then the next day there was a message for me from an Aunt Val with a telephone number, so I rang.
"Hello, I'm Karl. Can I speak to Val please."
"Yes, speaking. Do you remember me, I'm Victor's wife." "Yes, I spoke to you in Statford once."
"Your grandmother's o.k. Victor left home when he was sixteen and cut himself off from your grandmother after your grandfather died. Victor doesn't approve of some of the things she has done and he doesn't get on with your mother. He's quite frightened of her. Steven said to me that you had cancelled the meeting, I thought you were close to your grandmother."
"I'm not very good at guilt trips. Look, who's sick in this situation?"
"Who, your mother or your grandmother?"
"Just get yourselves together and then I will come down, Steven said that the weekend might be cancelled."
"Which weekend was it ?"
"This one.'
"The meeting was cancelled because Steven had seen your mother. Look, if you want to see your grandmother, go and see your grandmother."

That same evening I had an argument over the 'phone with Steven as to why he had seen my mother. "It wasn't me it was Elizabeth." "You had no right to do that."

I slammed the 'phone down.
Feeling that I'd just been dumped, I rang Victor. "Don't get involved, no one wanted to know you." "Is it possible to come to your house, so that I can see my grandmother?" "Yes."

Then I rang Steven back after I had calmed down. We talked
a little, then he said :
"I'll see you in the future."
I said goodbye.
The following day I rang Elizabeth.
"Are you going down ?"
"Yes."
"Steven was quite pleased with you after you had calmed down
and rang him back, I thought you were some nutcase, you frightened me"
"I love words, I love your ability to twist things."
"I don't even know you, you should have heard what your mother had said about you. She'd washed her hands of you."
Then she put the 'phone down.

I came down to Cardiff and rang Victor, he told me to go to my grandmother's house and wait for him to come. The moment I saw him in his car I knew it was him. That afternoon in the house we looked at grandmother's photo album. "She always talked about you, and no one wanted to know. Your mother just wanted you out and no one could understand it; one out of a family of five."

Then he looked at me : "You can see his mother in him."
He looked at Larry. "I knew it was him the moment he came though the door."
I thought *'he's lying, he didn't recognise me.'* He asked me how
I was. "Your n mother went to the funeral of an aunt and none of the women would speak to her. It was all about you again." He looked at a picture of my sister. "Francine is doing Law now."

Then we went off in the car to the hospital to see my
grandmother. "We'll have to see whether his mother has come over. I don't want an argument in front his grandmother."

We arrived at the hospital, Larry and Victor asked the nurse if anybody else had come. "Yes, a woman", said the nurse.
"That must have been your mother."

I went in to see my grandmother. She was sitting slumped over in a chair, sleeping by the bed, her hair had changed colour to a blond
dona dona. "That's just her way of resting," said Larry. Victor looked at all the cards on the on the window sill.

"What's this. Oh, it must be her urinal bag", I said.
Victor then went off saying he had people to pay from his business, soon after he had gone I came across to the bed and sat down.
"Hello, it's me, Karl."
I spoke into her ear but she didn't come round, I went down to get her a card to put with the others, then came back.
"It's Karl."
I spoke into her ear again but she didn't move, then I held her hand.
After some time I went back to my grandmother's house with
Larry on the bus.

That evening I argued with Larry over what had happened :
"Why didn't you inform my mother that I was coming, then there would have been no problem with meeting the others?"
"Where have you been for the past ten years?"
"Who gave my date of birth to my grandmother then?" "Maybe it was your mother. You can't call the others your brothers, they're just people that you grew up with, John's not your father."
I gave no reply.

"Elizabeth ran in here going though all the drawers, looking for the marriage certificate fro me and your grandmother. Then your mother threatened me with a solicitor's letter too, saying that I was interfering with her business. So Val rang her to put her straight on the matter, your mother told her that

she'd given you away years ago, and when your grandmother was in hospital years ago your father had asked her to get in contact with you."
I thought of what the Children's Home had said to me, and I thought *'Why couldn't he do it himself ?'*

I went to the toilet, sat down and cried. When I came out Larry said "Victor told me you should see your grandmother and then go."

I went out for a drink to clear my mind and spoke to Steven on the 'phone: "She looked quite at peace." "I'll see you in the future, goodbye."

That night I felt very secure in her house. She had a picture of a Christmas scene in the corner of the room. I remembered the time she had rung the Home to wish me a Happy Christmas; she had been thinking of me for all those years. Then I noticed a small picture of my grandfather in the other corner. I looked again at the photographs of my grandmother's family. There was a picture of my mother's house, my father standing by a big window with deep red curtains in the background. As I looked around at the family pictures, here in my grandmother's house, I thought *'she seems to be the most caring person in the family and the most shat upon.'*
At last I fell asleep.

Chapter Fifteen

When I got back to Worcester I rang my mother's house. My brother Paul answered.
"Whoever gave my grandmother my date of birth", I said, "was responsible for that situation, and it must have come from our house. I've said everything I need to say."
I put the 'phone down.

I went home to my flat feeling so frustrated with all that had gone on. I picked up a teapot and threw it across the room; it went through the skylight. I did not now whether my grandmother was alive or dead. I thought '*these people only contacted me because my grandmother had. They play their fucked up games on the telephone. They have done nothing for me in my life.*'
I thought of my mother saying that she had washed her hands of me, and my father who had done nothing to stop all this. What a bastard! That Home that he had kept me in.

Then I remembered what my grandmother had said in Stratford to me: "I will leave everything to you." Why was she doing this to me? It seemed that they just wanted me off the scene, did not want to listen to me. Somehow I knew inside that my grandmother was not going to die, not just then when they thought she would. '*She wrote to me, and I wrote to her,*' I thought, '*so I will stay until she dies. If I got off the scene now I would be a bastard, and if I stay on the scene then I'm a bastard too, because my parents don't want me to. It's a no-win situation in the circumstances.*' I sat down and cried. What a mess. Then I thought of what Victor had said to me in her house. I sat down and wrote my mother a letter telling her how devoted she was to keeping me out of the family. "Please don't feel you have anything to repay, this is part of your devotion."

That evening in the pub I sat crying, feeling very guilty about sending the letter off, thinking that after all, my mother had sent the Family Allowance for all those years, and I never knew. Maybe she did care! So I rang her up:
"Hello mother. I've seen my grandmother in the hospital. How are you?"
"O.K."
"Goodbye."
I put the 'phone down.

Some days later, wondering why Elizabeth had gone into my grandmother's house, I rang her up.

"Why did you go rushing into my grandmother's house and ransack it?" I was enraged; my grandmother wasn't even dead yet. "Your grandmother had a very shady past," she said. "And I know from various conversations that your mother had stolen and spent your grandfather's insurance in the past. I didn't want Larry to be left with nothing; I was looking for any documentation. When your grandmother collapsed at that great family party at Caerphilly, your uncle Victor thought she was drunk, and hurried her off the scene because she was an embarrassment to the family's respectability. Then your mother kept her in the car all night. She's cut herself off from us now."

We said our goodbyes. I could tell that Elizabeth suspected me of turning up to see my grandmother simply in the hope of money; she thought my mother was a crook; she knew my brother Shaun had done time for fraud; she thought I was of the same ilk.

A week later I rang her again.
"I'm coming down in a week or so, and if Steven wants to come out for a drink I'm happy to do that. I've sent my mother a letter about how she is so devoted to keeping me out of the family. I suppose now she will be getting in contact with us over that."
"Steven is carrying a lot of your mother's guilt. In some ways he identifies with you. I don't know how you've coped all these years. What's it been like for you?"
"Well, it's like knowing your family's out there but you can't get in contact with them. It's like mourning; you want to grieve but you can't because you know they're out there somewhere."
"Well, Steven might be working, you know what it's like having your own business, you have to work when you can."
"O.K. I'll give him a ring from my grandmother's house and see if he's free to come out."

Then I rang Larry and asked how my grandmother was.

"Still very much the same, kid; she's been moved by the family to a hospice, run by nuns."
"I'll be down in a week so I can see her there."

A week later I went down to Cardiff, to my grandmother's house, and rang Steven from there.
"He's out working but he might ring back later", said Elizabeth. Larry decided to ring. "No, Larry," she said, "he'd feel I'm pushing him."
Eventually Steven got home, rang up, and now the meeting for the drink was off. Then an argument broke out again.
"Another family wind-up", I said.
"It's because your mother might be at the hospital if we went on Sunday."
"Look, she's responsible for her feelings," I said, "and I'm responsible for mine. That's not a problem for me. If we meet then we meet and that's that."
Willy Monteiro's invaluable teachings were suddenly kicking into action for me in a real-life situation.

We caught the bus over to see my grandmother.
"You shouldn't tell your grandmother what's been happening, it will upset her," said Larry.

The hospice was run by nuns; not the same order as the ones who worked at Father Hudson's. The whole place had a friendly atmosphere.

I walked in to a communal lounge area, where my grandmother was sitting up in a high-seated chair, looking out of the window. Her hair seemed to be almost blonde; she was fully dressed. I went over and sat down in front of her, and Larry sat next to her. She looked at me and started to cry. I moved my head from side to side and smiled, thinking *'it's O.K. now, I'm here.'* Then she looked at my hair. I could tell at once, by an almost psychic connection, that she thought it was untidy, so I got up and went to the toilet and put it straight for her; then I came back and sat down. She looked at the flowers that were on the table next to me, and then at me. She did it again and then again.
"Are they yours?" I asked, trying to make conversation.
She looked at the T.V., then back at me.

I was wondering how much of her brain was working. "Stratford?" I said, wondering if her memory was functioning. She looked at the wall, and then at me. Did this mean that walls have ears, I wondered? "Of course she remembers Stratford," said Larry. "It's a real Agatha Christie mystery, this situation." I flinched and looked at him, remembering what he had said to me before coming in to see her. "She likes Agatha Christie," he added.

Fixing a Pavarotti tape that she had in her cassette recorder he put the earphones on her head. "I'll have to take it back to the library soon," he said. "Steven, Victor and Maria and his mother all know you're here." She moved her head to look at Larry for some time, as if she were angry with him. She looked outside to the garden, at a statue of Mary. I looked at it for a time, then looked back at her. There was an acceptance there; an acceptance of death. Then she looked at me, pulling her bottom lip down.

I understood how she felt. It was time for us to go. I stood up, went over to her and put my hand on her ear and rubbed it. Then as we were leaving she moved her head as if she wanted to talk to me and made some sounds as if she did not want me to go. "I understand, don't try to talk, I'll be back tomorrow," said Larry. Inside I felt *'he's a bastard to her.'*
As we left she twisted her head round as far as it would go until she couldn't move it any more. As if she could see right the way around the back of her.

Over the next few weeks I rang the Nursing Home to ask how my grandmother was. I also rang Larry. He was always going on about my mother being there visiting, in order to keep me away. And if he wasn't going on about my mother it would be about my grandmother's will.

I'd rung Val one day and tried to explain to her that my mother had been sending the Family Allowance to Father Hudson's all those years, that I didn't know, and the Children's Home had been lying to me about some things. But I don't think she listened.

Larry told me that everyone in the family had cut themselves off from one another, making it impossible to talk to anybody. So, I decided to cut myself off from him and rang the Nursing Home direct. I asked the nuns not to tell Larry that I was coming down to see my grandmother.

I came in to the Nursing Home one day, hoping to miss him but he came in as I was sitting with her. He hadn't even stood my card up, as if I didn't exist. He sat himself down next to her bed and got the radio out of the cabinet.
"I must get this tuned in, how long have you been here?" "Not long."
"Why are your brothers and sister not here?" I sighed.

He knew I couldn't answer that one, and there was my grandmother in the bed just looking at me, trying to make some sound with her mouth. Feeling the frustration of not being able to say a thing to each other about what was going on. "Maybe they don't care."
He knew that I couldn't get in contact with my mother or father, or my brothers and sister.

After some time he decided to go. "I think I'll stay a little longer," I said. Then he started to argue, pushing me to the door while my grandmother sat looking at the scene. "Just go, are you mad or summat?" He clearly couldn't stand the emotional intensity of the situation; and really, neither could I.

I gave no reply and walked out of the building with him following.
"Are you coming to the bus with me?" "You go your way and I will go mine", I said, and he walked off.

I got home feeling so frustrated with what had happened over the past months, about all the family. I decided to go to the solicitors.
"They can't stop you from seeing your grandmother without a court order."

I rang Elizabeth. "I have been told to get off the scene on two occasions. My grandmother wrote to me and I wrote back to her and that is that. As far as I'm concerned it's nothing to do with you, or with my mother. I'm not having any more of this rubbish. If any of you interfere any further I'm taking legal action. I will do it. I have said everything that I need to say to you." I put the 'phone down.

A week later while I was sitting in my grandmother's room with her my mother came into the room. We looked at each other in silence. I found I was no longer afraid of her; once again Willy Monteiro's teaching came in to play.

As it were from outside, I was able to see the three chief characters in this psychodrama; what was going to happen?

My mother came across to the other side of the bed and put her keys down. Imprinted on my mind was the interview with Mrs. Bellamy; did I have 'a desire to kill my mother with a knife'? No, or I would have done it years ago. So that analysis was wrong; the picture changed on its axis. And what had Victor said to me in the house? 'Your grandmother always talked about you; no-one else would.' His words echoed in my head and they echo through my life. *Inside I felt I wanted to reach out to my mother and tell her 'it's O.K.'*

"Hello mother," she said. She stroked her cheek. "She's probably tired," she said. "I'll come back tomorrow."
She came around to the other side of the bed. "She just opened her eyes," I said. She was standing very close to me.
"She's very tired now, she's been up today," said my mother.
Then she walked to the door and made some small talk with the other people in the room. "Oh, my keys."
I reached my hand across the bed and placed the keys on the other side for her to pick up. She came across and picked them up. "Thank you."
"It's my pleasure."
She looked at my grandmother again, then left the room.

This whole scene seemed like something taking place in a war zone. A moment of calm and stillness, of 'silenzio', almost of acceptance, between the three of us, three generations on a battle-field.

I got up and went over to the window sill and looked at my grandmother's cards. Seeing a picture of my grandfather there I turned it to face her, then came over to her and asked her if she wanted me to come again.
"If you do, will you blink?" She blinked a lot.

I didn't know whether she understood or not. I thought she looked so nice there, just like a child. I said, "I remember the time you rang me up to wish me a Happy Christmas." She blinked. I left the room, thinking *'she means come back in a few days.'* As I left, I realized she had a slight warm orange glow about her.

Chapter Sixteen

Back home in Worcester a week later I rang the hospice and asked one of the nuns how my grandmother was getting on.
"She's been moved," she said.
"What? Where to?"
"A rest home; didn't your family tell you? I told them you were devoted to her."
"I'm afraid it's all part of a family feud, sister."

Feeling confused I rang Larry.
"Haven't you heard? I asked your family to get in touch with you."
"No, I haven't heard anything."
"Well, she woke up with a pain in the chest."
"And?"
"So they gave her morphine, she had a heart attack and then she died."

I'd so much hoped that she'd live long enough to get the power of speech back, and maybe we could all have had a civilized conversation, instead of playing stupid games.
"Oh, I'm very sorry," I said. "When is the funeral? This Thursday? I'll see you tomorrow then; I'm going to ring Steven."

I put the 'phone down, feeling very shocked. That's the end, then, I thought; that's the end of an era. That's the end of finding out why she contacted me in the first place; now I shall never know what she thought or what she knew. And I could never explain to her what had happened to me; how Father Hudson's had lied to me and what my life had been like. I'd hoped that she might have been the link between myself and my parents. This might have been a completely false hope, but now I had lost it altogether. Now any contact I made would have to be on my own.

I rang Steven. "I'm sorry about your mother," I said.
"Well it was expected. I've told the others that I'm just having me and Elizabeth and the kids here after the funeral. So I don't know what you'll be doing then." This made things quite clear.
"I'll probably go to Larry's house."
I said goodbye.

I went to the pub. Then the fact the she was dead really sank in and I cried. The following day I went to buy some clothes for the funeral, but each time I walked into a shop I started to cry and then just walked out in a daze. Part of this was guilt on my part; I felt guilty that I hadn't made more contact or tried harder.

I tried to get the train down to Cardiff but in my grief I caught the wrong one and had to change at Bristol. On the way to my grandmother's house I got myself some clothes for the funeral, and bought myself a copy of the South Wales Echo. It was full of obituaries of my grandmother written by my family. My name was never mentioned in the lists of grandchildren, as if I didn't exist. I'd been airbrushed out.

Reaching my grandmother's house I saw all the cards that friends of my grandmother had sent to Larry. A friend of theirs from Stratford had sent a card. I was impressed by the number of friends she had made, and realized how little I really knew about her life. I told Larry what Steven had said to me over the 'phone.
"I thought we were all going over to his place," he said.
'More of their games,' I thought to myself.
He rang Steven.
'He didn't want me there,' I thought, *'that's why he said that, and none of them even contacted me to say she was dead.'*

After Larry had put the 'phone down he talked about the will and seemed quite pleased with himself.
"She signed this a week before she died. Steven and Grace, your grandmother's niece, are the executors."
Then he passed it over to me. I looked at it for some time. It was all written in legal jargon and very hard to understand. I thought to myself: *'why did Elizabeth come ransacking the house to find out if Larry and my grandmother were married if Steven was the executor of the will? She'd have known all about it. Maybe she was afraid grandmamma was going to write another will in my favour. Steven had never had any intention of coming out for a drink with me.'*

That same evening Larry introduced me to a friend of my grandmother, Annette, who lived around the corner from her. She was my age and she had lived in Care too. She had cut marks all over her arms. She told me of her experiences in a mental hospital; she had not been able to come to terms with the fact that she had had a handicapped child, who had died at the same time that my grandmother was in the hospice. We discovered that we had quite a lot in common with each other, both having been in Care and understanding the way people were treated in institutions. She told me a lot about my grandmother. Some things I already knew about, and some I didn't.

"She knew she was going to die. She would go to the church and sometimes come in here to see me afterwards, and she'd be crying. She told me that she'd had a bellyful of her children's problems over the years, but she felt very guilty that she'd put your mother onto the street when Francine was only a baby." I knew there had been disapproval there of my father; I remembered my grandmamma saying that she had told my mother 'you've made your bed and you must lie in it.' "Your grandmother told me about things that she did to the others, too," said Annette. "She said your mother used to put you out into the cold as a child; even on Christmas Day. She'd been looking for you for about a year or so. She changed her will, didn't she Larry?" Larry sat there saying nothing, just taking it all in.
I wondered why it took her so long to find me, and thought to myself *why didn't Larry tell me she was looking for me all those months ago? It would have made life so much easier for me.*

"Your mother could be quite vindictive; she told me not to go around to see your grandmother," said Annette.
"Yes, she's put a message in the paper saying 'much loved by Francine, Sean and Paul.'
"I bet that hurt."
"Yes."
"Your grandmother said you used to call her grandmamma. Your aunt Maria wanted to look after you, your grandmother said, when you were little." But my aunt Maria was only young when I went into care; she'd have been far too young to look after a child.
"Will you come to the funeral tomorrow to give me some support?" I asked.
"Yes."

"Thank you."

It had got late so I went back with Larry and went to bed. I found that I could not sleep so I looked at some of the family photographs and finally fell asleep at dawn, to be woken all too soon by Larry. The day was cold and wet. Annette came round with her friend and we waited for the funeral car. When it arrived we all got in and drove to the Funeral Chapel. It felt strange; I had never been to a place like this before. There were some old people already there, and the coffin at the front with all the flowers at one side of it. I walked over to see if I could see a wreath from my mother. Yes, there it was. I sat down in the front row with Larry and Annette and a friend of hers. It was the first family funeral I had ever been to, and I felt very nervous.

Elizabeth came in with Steven. He came over to where I was sitting, shook my hand and sat down beside me. Elizabeth went across to Larry who was standing looking at the coffin and put her arm around him. I thought to myself *what a creep*. She came back with Larry who sat by me, then Victor sat down with us. We looked at each other hard, as if to say 'you bastard' to each other. Elizabeth sat behind me.

"Is that you Karl?" she said. I turned and there was Val. I saw Maria come in and sit down, *'I recognise both of you,'* I thought; but I couldn't have seen them since I was three. I looked at Elizabeth, thinking to myself *'as if she didn't know who I was.'* But I do look very like Shaun, so perhaps she was confused?

"Yes," I replied.
Then Elizabeth turned to Annette and her friend:
"Can you go over to the other side? This side's for the family."
They both got up and went over to the other side of the chapel; I felt very much abandoned. Then the service started and ten minutes into it my mother walked in with my father and sister and her friend. Victor turned and looked at Larry.
"She's late."

The sermon began. The priest talked about families, so I leaned forward deliberately to listen and so that the others could see me listening; when he finished I leaned back and sang the next hymn.

Twenty minutes later the service was over and we all made our way to the door. A friend of my mother's said "Hello Karl." "Hello," I replied. I wondered who the hell she was? So my mother's friends could acknowledge me but she couldn't?

It was cold outside and raining. My mother was standing not far from the door with my father and sister. None of them spoke to me. I thought to myself *'I'm not standing here like a lemon, it's too cold.'* and made my way to the car with Larry and Annette and her friend and got in the front seat. Steven came across and opened the door.
"This is for the family only."

I sat there saying nothing and watched Annette and her friend walk up the road with their umbrella in the rain. Looking through the window with the raindrops on it I felt sorry for them but could do nothing. I started to feel quite frightened and looked across to where my parents stood with my sister. My mother's back was against the car. My sister looked across trying to avoid eye contact with me. My father's hair was greying a little since I had seen him last. He was talking to my mother. Then my father looked towards the car and gave me a little smile. I felt much better for that; my sister looked across too but quickly looked away. Victor and Maria had got into the car with Steven, and Larry was still in the back.

I could just about hear the three of them talking, asking the driver whether this funeral car was part of a family business. Then I looked away to the hearse; its number plate was JP something. Victor started talking to the driver about family feuds, and the driver told him a story about someone that had smashed the window of one of their cars in a family feud. "Um ... Justice of the Peace" said Victor.
"More like John Player Special," said Steven, looking over towards my parents. I thought he'd allowed himself to say that because my father had smiled at me. "Trust you to think of that", said Victor. "It's just like royalty," he went

on. Was this because I was sitting in the front? I felt this was some kind of coded insult.

In silence I thought back to the 'phone call to Elizabeth, about them trying to kick me out of the hospital; that's why they are going on like this, I thought, they don't know how to handle the situation. The car started up and drove past Llandaff cathedral. "And there's Llandaff cathedral", said Victor, as if I didn't know.

For the rest of the journey I listened to them making stupid remarks until we came to the graveyard and got out in the rain to watch my grandmother being buried. Larry stood at the graveside: "It's like a dream," he said, as he looked down at the coffin. He was weeping.

We stood there for a minute or two then got back in the car. Steven gave directions to the driver to go to his house, and ten minutes later we arrived. It was a large house in the suburbs of Llandaff; very desirable. I glimpsed Elizabeth closing the door and running upstairs. I got out and walked up the path to the door with the others. Elizabeth came down the stairs with a towel in her hand and put it where I was about to put my feet. "I don't want any mud in the house," she said, as if expecting something really filthy. The message was very clear.

I could see my sister in the kitchen, so I wiped my feet and walked towards her. "Greetings." "Hello," she said, looking me up and down. I felt intensely nervous by now, thinking *what am I doing here?*' I went into the lounge and helped myself to a whisky from a table with food on it, sat down on a chair and lit up a cigarette to stop myself from shaking. *'If I'm holding something I might not feel so frightened,'* I thought. I looked around the room and noticed the old people from the church. On the wall was a picture of a copper holding a crook by the scruff, illuminated by a lamp. Clearly there was some symbolism here; in every crook there's a copper, I thought, and in every copper there's a crook. Where did all this money come from?

Just then Francine came in and asked if anybody wanted coffee. "Yes please", I replied, with some of the others.

I looked around to see if there was an ashtray, but there wasn't one in sight so I got up and went into the kitchen. Elizabeth stood there.
"Have you an ashtray?" I asked, holding the ash in my hand.
"I don't want any trouble from you," she said, shaking her finger at me like an overbearing parent. I ignored this comment and asked again: "Have you an ashtray?"
"Did you hear what I said?"
"Yes," I said. She handed me an ashtray and I went back into the other room. Larry, Steven, Victor and all the others who'd come to the funeral were there except for my parents; their absence was very noticeable. My sister Francine went across and kissed Larry, then came back and handed me a coffee. I wanted her support in some way. After I'd finished my cigarette I went across and asked her for a plate.

"My parents want to speak to you," she said, "so long as you can speak to them sensibly. They find you hostile; you can't force people to do things they don't want to do," she said. (This was exactly what Father Tucker had said to me long after my breakdown…..had there been some point of contact between them, then?)

"Oh, you mean they're sensible now."
This didn't go down well. "You're talking about people I've known all my life," she said.
I said nothing. She handed me a plate at arm's length, I got myself some pizza (the Italian touch) and sat down next to Val. She introduced me to her two children, I said hello and shook their hands. Maria handed Val some photographs of her children "Can I have a look?" I asked.
Val handed them to me.
"I've seen these before at Larry's house."

I handed them back. Larry sat there all alone while Victor talked about some photographs of my grandfather: "That's Aunty May's wedding. That must have been one of the biggest weddings I can remember."
I thought to myself *'I always wanted to know who that woman was in the background of that picture.'*

Val turned to me:

"Well here's the family if you want it."
I said nothing.
She looked over to where my sister was sitting.
"She's very like your mother was years ago."

I looked at Val and felt that I liked her. Steven was by the table; he turned to me but I turned away deliberately and picked up the plate that I had put on the floor feeling *'I don't need you.'* I felt I needed a drink of orange so I went into the kitchen, Maria was there.
"Well, here's the family, we're not all the same," she said.
I didn't know what to say, so I got my drink, went next door and sat down again.

Val introduced me to an older woman there; a great-aunt.
"We're from the poorer end of the family," said the great aunt, "there are the richer ones", she said pointing to my uncles Victor and Steven, and to Maria.
"Your grandmother took all the money, that's why they're all so greedy now. If George was alive this would never have happened to you, he was very strict."
George was my true grandfather, my mother's father.

My sister came across and crouched down next to me:
"You're living in the past."
I looked her straight in the eyes.
"If you want to talk to my parents," she said "just go and see them."
"All right, I'll meet them on neutral territory."
She got up and moved away from me. Val had been sitting there listening to it all, then another female relative came up to Val and started to talk:
"I was a bit of a bastard myself in Barnardo's." She shook hands like a wet fish.

I knew the comment was directed at me so I said nothing, Val smiled. Most of the people had left by then. Francine decided to go so I said goodbye. Steven took Larry and me back to my grandmother's house. After we'd been dropped off Larry took away all the cards from around the room. I rang Annette and said that I was sorry but that I couldn't have done a thing to make sure that she and her friend got a lift.

The following day I went back to Worcester wondering whether or not to ring my mother. In the end I did.
"Hello?"
"Who am I speaking to?"
"Your father."
"Can I speak to my mother?"
"She's in the bath; I'll go and call her."
She came to the 'phone.
"Hello."
"Hello, that's a good start," I said, reflecting on some past acrimonious exchanges.

"Why did all this have to happen?" she asked.
It's karmic unfinished business, I thought, and I replied "Because you needed it."

"Coleshill were lying to me," I told her.
"Why would they lie to you?"
"Because", I said, "they believe that the set of problems that a person has as a child are the same set of problems they have as an adult. Also, they wrapped me up in bureaucratic red tape, so they must have done it to you too. If I'd been adopted that would have been that. All this would never have happened - "

"If I can get a word in edgeways," she interrupted, "while your grandmother was dying the family were all playing one off against the other, it was like psychodrama. And that funeral was a farce. I wish you hadn't gone; they were all laughing at you. Francine despised her you know, and Steven only lived here because he felt neglected at Victor's. I don't know why he did that to me. And that Annette didn't even know her."

Part of me felt sorry for her; clearly the whole family had been criticizing her for years and she was hopelessly confused. I wanted to understand the confusion. But on the other hand, over all those years she hadn't made any effort to clarify the situation. The situation needed her input to be redeemed. So maybe, I thought, in a karmic sense not only did she need what had happened to her, but the situation needed her for any satisfactory resolution. She needed it, and it needed her.

"I don't know Annette really either," I said. "But I know the rest of them, I can see through them like glass. Victor said that you'd gone to the funeral of a great-aunt and none of the women would speak to you."
"That's not true, I helped to get that funeral together, and Valerie was partly responsible for me having a breakdown. And John was an alcoholic." I wondered about this. I remembered that Barbara Bellamy said there was a psychiatric report on my mother at the time of my being taken into care; how Valerie was partly responsible was a mystery. This was a very intense family; once again I felt I was on the outside looking in.

"Can I speak to my father?"
"Yes."
She handed over to him; this was the first time we'd ever had a conversation on the phone
"Why didn't you want me at a children's home in Cardiff?" This was a very perplexing issue for me; why did they send me so far away? Had it been pressure from Father Hudson's, or from my parents? I needed some clarification.
"I don't remember that ...."
I thought *you're lying.'*
"Why didn't you want me adopted?"
"I was hoping that things would work out."

Can this be true? I asked myself. Can a father really resign all responsibility like this? The question of illegitimacy reared its head in my mind again.

"How is Sean?" I asked.
"He's in Southampton."
"And what's he doing?"
"He's a mason."
"I don't like masons. That was a joke...."

Chapter Seventeen

Soon after we'd finished speaking I rang up Miss Carroll.

"My grandmother was trying to put the family together before she died. Would you ask Father Tucker to say a Mass for her please, he was close to my family."

"You will have to write to the Archbishop's house," she answered obscurely. What did this mean?

Presently I learned from Paul Wright my childhood friend that at this very time, 1990, Father Tucker had been exposed by the Birmingham Post as having had a love child, and had fled the diocese. He had fathered a daughter, Sian, in 1989, and signed her birth certificate. Mrs Gill Devlin, a divorcee, claimed that he had lived with her and their daughter as a family for eighteen months, having first embarked on an affair with her while he was her parish priest at Cannock. By 1992 she was anxious to trace him to claim more alimony from him (he was already paying £15 a week), but the Archbishop of Birmingham, the Most Reverend Couve de Murville, confirmed that at that time neither he personally, nor the Diocesan Offices, had any knowledge of Father Tucker's whereabouts.

(The Sunday Mercury presently tracked him down to a 'coloured ghetto' parish in Port Elizabeth in South Africa in 1996. He eventually emerged from hiding and tried to pursue a libel claim against five Irish newspapers whom he claimed had damaged his reputation in the way they reported the affair. He also claimed that he had been allowed to return to the ministry after deeply repenting and asking God for forgiveness)

From my own perspective, this news was very confusing. On the one hand, I now knew that Tucker was not always a wholly honest man; he had been leading a double life for some years while holding the position of parish priest at Cannock. He could have left the church and done work of a similar nature as a layman, but he didn't. On the other hand, perhaps his experience gave him a broader perspective on human life and social work, and one could see him as being simply ahead of his time. There is no biblical ruling against the marriage of church leaders, and in fact the Catholic Church did not insist on priestly celibacy until the 11th century.

He had left Father Hudson's in about 1984, when the Society decided to appoint a lay director, Mr Pinches.

But at the time I did not know all this. I continued my conversation with Joyce Carroll.
"My mother wants to see me," I said.
"How do you feel about that?"
I gave no reply, thinking '*I'm not playing that one. I'm not doing any more transactional analysis thank you.*'

"I can understand that you'd always wanted to get in contact with your parents, but you were disturbed, in Care." *My NLP work with Willie Monteiro kicked in again.* "The set of problems that you ascribe to people aren't worth having," I said. "If you gave people problems that were worth having ...." but before I could say 'then you might improve the quality of their lives' she slammed the 'phone down. I had beaten them at their own game.

Some days later I rang my mother and left her a message. Her response to this was to relay my own message back to me; very disconcerting.

"I forgot to make an appointment to see you," I said bitterly.
 "You could come down on Thursday," she responded. Maybe this was the beginning of a breakthrough?

But she went on to say "If you were down and out Victor wouldn't help." *What did this have to do with anything*, I wondered? My problem was nothing to do with Victor; it was to do with her and my father.

"I wish things had worked out for you years ago," she said.
"I feel bitter about the way that I was treated."
"I think you're a very sarcastic person. I think you tried to push your way into the family."
I gave no reply.
"I made a promise to my grandmother in Stratford that I would look after her when she was dying," I told her.
"And now she's dead" my mother said abruptly, as if I was the guilty party, "and how did you look after her?"

"A promise is a promise. Why did my father do nothing? Because he never does a bloody thing. And why did you ring me up all those years ago when I was seventeen?"
She slammed the 'phone down. I rang again and this time my father answered. "Don't upset your mother," he said brusquely. No, I thought, that's how this whole family works; don't upset the mother.

However, some days later I thought to myself, *'If she said she wanted to see me then I will see her.'* So I went down to Cardiff, to her house. I knocked and she came to the door.
"I didn't say you could come here, but you'd better come in now. There's not a lot I can tell you."
I went into the front room. My father stood in front of the T.V. I looked around. There was a fish tank in the corner, and a picture of Steven.
"Oh, goldfish."
"Tropical," said my father.

We walked into the kitchen, and there was another picture of Steven. We sat down. It felt strange seeing them together.
"I've got a picture of him in every room."
She looked at it and almost went into a trance.
My father turned and pointed at my mother:
"Now don't you get upset," he said.
He looked at me, got up and went out of the room. My mother and I sat there looking at each other.

"He's going to work now. I'm going up to change."
Some time later she came down and made a coffee. She went into the conservatory by the kitchen.
"We had this done last year."
We sat down; it was a beautiful summer evening.
"I don't know why she did that to me," she said.
She seemed to be searching her mind.
"When Francine was born she kicked us out. John went to his mothers', but she didn't like me, so I stayed on friend's floors. I'd be drying nappies on the pram, the one with the big wheels", she said, rotating her arms like wheels.
"I know the ones. We used them as trolleys in the Home."

"Then I met a cousin who said there was a place in Bradford," she went on, "so I went up there. The room was very expensive for those days. I didn't know anybody. When you were born in the hospital Francine went to touch you on the cheek and John shouted at her. Then he said 'I'm going to leave you now.' You started to cry and I just said 'no'. I know it's cruel to say so but it's almost as if I didn't have you. There was no Family Allowance in those days; it was mental cruelty. It was just me he wanted; when each child was born he would leave. If I could have divorced him then there would have just been you and Francine and the others would never have been born. There was someone", she said, shaking her head "but now...."

"And the priest?"

"I thought that he would understand. John would always go on about you as if you were the only one he cared about. I couldn't accept you back because of his drinking. I had to get the doctor in here once to reason with him because he was so drunk. He's got good insight into people, though Francine's sharper he says. Watch Elizabeth, she's trouble. She goes from one branch of the family to the other getting into their business. And I know something about Victor, and he would be quite surprised if he thought that I knew. But I'm not going to say. Well, you said that you can see through them like glass."

Just then Paul came in through the front door.
"Don't tell him", she whispered.
"Look who's here", she called to Paul.
He came in looking a little nervous and sat down.

My mother stood up. "I'm going to watch some telly," she announced, and went next door. All evening we talked about my brother and sister; things we had done and the Home and how they were lying and then lying about their lies, until it was very late.

"What was she talking about? I remember your name being mentioned a lot when I was little."
I repeated to him what she had told me, then she came back in. "Would it be possible to stay the night?" I asked.

"You should have thought of that before."
Paul looked at me and I looked at him
"He can sleep in my room."
"No."
"I'll sleep in here."
"O.K. then."
She got some bedclothes from upstairs and put them down for me, then we went next door to watch the telly while my mother went to bed.

"It's quite strange staying in your family home." Paul looked at me. "Yes."
My father came in at two, stood in front of the telly and smiled, and then went out again.
"Strange." I said.
"He never comes in here if I'm here."
"Very twisted."
Then my mother came in: "Come on, break it up."
Paul and I went to bed.

The following day my mother drove me into town.
"Sometimes mothers only get in contact with their children in Homes for their money. I don't agree with that," she said.
I said nothing, thinking that it didn't matter.
"Why did you keep my grandmother in the car all night?"
"At that party Victor told me to get her into the car because she was a disgrace. And then three of them put her into the car and left me to look after her."

She showed me where all her friends were as we drove though the town. After that she dropped me off, and I got the train back to Worcester. For the following week I was thinking of my father and wondering why he hadn't wanted me in Cardiff. I rang him, but my mother answered.
"Can I come down to see my father? There's something I want to say to him."
"You know what he's like; it's in one ear and out the other one." "Well, nevertheless, once I've said it, I've said it."
"You can't force people to do what they don't want to do," she said. "I'm not forcing anybody to do anything they don't want to do." "He's getting dressed at the moment. I'll call him and ask if he wants to see you."

He came to the 'phone.
"Can I come down to see you?" "Yes."

The following day I went down to Cardiff and arrived at the house late. My mother opened the door. "We're all going out soon, but come in, we're having dinner. John was saying that your grandmother contacted you over an argument."
I thought to myself *'that must have been because of the argument we had over the 'phone after her death. They seem to be blaming her for all their problems instead of themselves.'*

"What did you want to say to John?" "It doesn't matter now."
After we had finished dinner my mother drove into town. I went over to Larrys', stayed the night, then went back to see my father. Seeing him through the window I knocked on the glass. He got up and came to the door and let me in.
"Did you stay at Larry's?" he asked.
"Yes. Can I have a coffee?"
"Yes, I was just waiting for your mother to come back." He went into the conservatory.
"I'm not going to stay long."
I came in and sat down opposite him.
"You didn't keep me in Care because of love. That was spite, I know."
"You know fuck all."
He threw his arms forward, shouting: "What do you know?"

He moved his head to one side as if to listen to what I had to say. I was thinking to myself *'my mother was right.'* I felt a little shocked.

"I didn't have a good mother," he said.
"Yes, I thought you would have known better."
"We're not all kings and gods. All this is an embarrassment to me. I suppose we have to live with this for the rest of our lives. We've all got skeletons in cupboards; Victor almost got nicked for stealing, and Steven and Elizabeth are the same."

"Yes I know; she was in Larry's house looking to see if Larry was married, so I know what they're like. Didn't my grandmother want to look after me?"
"She couldn't look after her fucking self. She never worried about bills and Steven lived in a caravan with her until he went to live at Victor's. He came to live here because he felt unwanted by them."
He moved forward to scratch his leg; there were scabs on his leg. "What's that?" I asked, "is it from your boots at work?" No answer.

I stood up.
"Can I borrow a fiver from you? I need it for hitching home." He looked at me.
"I'm not like Sean. I'll give it you back."
He gave me the fiver.
"What's the best way to hitch a lift from here?"
We both went to the door; he opened it and looked from left to right. I stepped out and he showed me the way.
"See those people holding cards up?"
Pointing down the road he waved his hands in the air as if he was hitching, then moved back into the house looking from right to left again. As he closed the door, walking away I thought about what I'd just done. I walked to the place he'd pointed out and waited for a lift back to Worcester.

Later I began thinking about what he'd said to me that day, and about the way he'd acted outside, looking to see if the neighbours were watching. And what my mother had said to me, 'it was only me he wanted.' I sent him back the fiver in a birthday card, thinking about what he'd said over the 'phone.
"I'm your father, so Coleshill was right."

Some days later I gave him a ring. My mother answered the 'phone. "Hello?" I shouted down the 'phone. "I've never met such a spiteful, vindictive-minded bastard in all my life and all this in our own back yard. Would you tell him that?"
"What?" "Just tell him that."
I rang Victor.
"Hello." "Victor ?" "Speaking."
"My father visited the Children's Home when I was nine. He told the nuns that he wanted me to live in Cardiff. But on the records at the Children's

Home it said that he didn't want me there. That means when he came up to visit he was just taking the piss out of me. He did that to be spiteful to my mother. I've cut myself off from them now."

"The only way you can get your own back on them is to make some money. If you were down and out they wouldn't help you."

Chapter Eighteen

Some days later, feeling pissed off with all the family, I rang Miss Carroll.
"I've broken my skylight and I've got an eviction order. Well, I wanted to get away from Worcester anyway."
"Oh don't leave Worcester, you've got all your friends there."
"I suppose that Father Tucker was trying to protect me. I think I'm going to write a book about all this." When he initially talked to me at Father Hudson's, he was definitely lying, but probably with good intentions.
"I suppose now you're going to get obsessed about your writing." She only said that because I'd been to a Special School; they never let you forget it.

I rang Annette.
"Did my grandmother ever get in contact with a Children's Home?"
"Yes, she got in contact with a Catholic Home in Birmingham about fifteen months before she died. She also tried the Samaritans."
"Thank you very much."
I thought of Coleshill. *'Why are they lying to me?'* I asked myself. *'Why did they say I was eighteen months old when I was nearly four? Why did they plant the idea of illegitimacy in my head.......?'* Every lie had led to more questions than answers.

I rang Mr Pinches.
"Did my grandmother get in contact with you fifteen months before she died? It's about her will."
"Ah!" he said. "There was an incident only last week where somebody had wanted to contact someone else and we passed the message on." He implied that they *always* passed messages on.
I thought, *'either he's lying, or they were grossly inefficient.'*
"As an institution, Father Hudson's abused me."
"To the best of my knowledge we didn't, but I can't change your beliefs."
"If I could get you in a courtroom for what you did to me I would. If I'd had the right information at the right time about my mother things would have worked out years ago. According to Mrs. Bellamy, the reckless way you re-introduced me to my parents meant I would or will kill my mother with a knife. You psychologically abused me."
He reframed my reply, "And you're abusing me."

"The only reason you arranged that interview with Mrs. Bellamy," I went on, "is that Father Tucker had left by the back door after he had caused all that damage by telling me that I was put into Care at eighteen months old. All you say is 'your parents are shit and we are so wonderful'."
I slammed the 'phone down.

I thought I would ask again and rang him again.
"I want to know; did my grandmother get in contact with you? I know she got in contact years ago and you told her to fuck off, but did she get in contact fifteen months before she died?"
"I will ask."
"Thank you."
Some days later I rang him again.
"Yes I've spoken to Miss Carroll and she said yes, your grandmother did get in contact years ago."
"Oh, what a nice cover-up."
"Karl, Karl."
"I can be clever too." Remembering what Father Tucker had said, that the records were 'fragmented', I asked
"Can I have a look at those fragmented records?"
"Yes".
I slammed the 'phone down once more.

I thought *was fifteen months years ago? Was the early eighties years ago? What was years ago? A nice mental loop. It's a pattern-stopper; Miss Carroll had been trying to avoid my question.*

Some time later I rang and spoke to one of the social workers.
"Can I speak to Miss Carroll?" "She's in a meeting at the moment, can I give her a message?" "Yes, just tell her I wasn't disturbed *in* Care, I was disturbed *by* her care. This is called reframing by telephone. It's an Ericksonian strategy, he was a psychiatrist in the 1950s, this technique was used by him." "Can she ring you back?" "No."

I rang Mr. Pinches again. "I watched my grandmother die. She couldn't talk. You knew the opportunity was there, I wanted to talk to her about all the things that had gone on in the past, all that misunderstanding. But she was

unable to talk, and I was unable to talk to her, and there she was with her urinal bag and I just watched her die and neither of us could talk to each other. How do you feel about that? You always ask me how I feel."
"Oh well...."
I put the 'phone down.

Some months later I rang Miss Carroll.
"I've been doing some writing about my experiences in Care and I would like to be able to look at some school reports. Is that possible?"
"Yes."
1 felt confused and frightened; *she's stopped me in the past, why is she letting me look at them now?'*
"Are you in a writing club?"
"No."
"I'll make a note of it in my diary. What's the best date for you?"
"April 16th."
"I'll confirm that for you in writing."

No letter came and presently I fell ill. I decided I would play them at their own game. I thought the best way of doing this would be to write them a letter without letting on that I didn't trust them. If I sent a letter it meant that I didn't trust them anyway.

I rang Mr. Pinches to say that I could not come up on the 16th because I was ill.
"I have bursitis." "That's tennis elbow, not the knee." I'd thought he wouldn't know what it was. "So what's the best time for you to come up. Maybe the 29th or the 30th?" "Yes that seems O.K." "I'll tell Miss Carroll."
"Thank you."

Then I wrote a letter:

Dear Miss Carroll,
I am writing to confirm that I was unable to keep our appointment, in connection with me having access to my records in the children's home, of the 16th April due to the fact that I was ill. I have spoken to the director and he has made a further appointment for the 29th/ 30th April 1991.

As this arrangement was made over the telephone I would appreciate it if you would write to confirm the appointment.
Yours in anticipation,
Karl A. Bicknell.

No reply came. I rang Miss Carroll again. She was busy so I asked the receptionist, "What time would it be best for me to come up?" I waited while she went away to ask somebody. "Do you want to come in the morning or the afternoon?" "I think the afternoon would be the best time for me, thank you." I said good bye and put the 'phone down.

It was four in the afternoon when I arrived at the Social Workers Office. I rang the doorbell and was let into the old playroom. I looked around. There was still a Scandinavian landscape over the fireplace that had been there when I was in Care; it brought back a lot of memories... I felt thoroughly drained. I asked myself why I was doing this. I'd been through the whole experience of meeting my parents and my whole family; I'd been through extensive psychotherapy; I knew now who I was, and all I wanted to do now was to write about my life. But I needed the records for accuracy.

Presently Miss Carroll walked into the room with my records in her hand, looking me up and down.
"I said two o'clock." This threw me for a moment. Nobody had mentioned a time to me.
I sat down.
"I have to go at five, can you come back later?"
"Yes."
"Can you come back tomorrow?"
"Yes."

"If you're doing some writing you'll have to ask your mother." She sat down at the long table and passed me a thick folder of papers. I sat on the far side of the table from her and opened the records. I felt very vulnerable. I picked up a letter from my mother and started to read it.
"It's my mother writing to send the Family Allowance."
I picked up the letter and started to read, feeling very nervous with Miss Carroll in the room.

"You're reading them in reverse. You don't trust us? Give it to me, you're racing through it." *This triggered the memory of my first contact with my mother, when Father Tucker had said I was 'steamrollering it'.*
"You need somebody to interpret it for you."

She took the records from me.
"Your mother writes in an intelligent hand. Here's a letter from your mother asking for you to be moved to Cardiff."
I could see a note at the top of the letter, written in pencil: "whatever for?" *'Why in pencil?' I thought*. So my father had nothing to do with this, then. It had been nothing to do with my father, then; nothing at all.
She laughed.
"Oh, May Fallen, 'whatever for.' She must have thought 'what is she doing now?' You can understand that. Your mother was unstable. There must have been a case conference about that." *Did this mean that I myself was unstable?*

She put the letter down without reading it and without looking at me. She just looked at the file.
"There are bits of my own past that I don't understand," she said. "I suppose that's why I can identify with you, because I was in care too." *She was re-anchoring her earlier remarks when I had revisited Father Hudson's.* I thought *'I know myself.'*
"Those fragmented records...."
'Clever,' I thought, remembering when I'd asked Mr. Pinches for those same records and what Father Tucker had told me years before about them being incomplete.

Suddenly she dropped a bombshell. "John was not your biological father."
I was shocked. Could this be true?
"The nuns told us nothing," I said.
"They were not allowed to in those days. Do you want a hanky? You were deprived. Oh, I must say that you should have been adopted. That's my maternal instinct coming out."

She pointed to herself, looking at me, and went on to read a letter.

"A health visitor came to find you in a room with no clothes on and your mother told her that she didn't buy you clothes. She said that you used to shout at her. But you shout at us now and you're adult." Was she implying that because my mother was mentally unhinged, I myself was mentally unhinged, and that was why I shouted? She certainly implied that my protests were unwarranted. Was she using transactional analysis? Was she assuming that the patterns set up by my mother would be repeated in my own psyche? She may have been using neuro-linguistic-programming techniques too, to anchor her own beliefs in me.

She read out another letter:
"I collected Karl today. His mother had put a blanket over him because she did not want the neighbours to see him. His mother writes to say that the neighbours were asking about Karl."
Then she read:
"*Karl's father came to the nursery and Karl did not recognize him. He gave the children some sweets, and he said that he did not want to impose himself. I walked Mr Bicknell to the bus stop and he was shaking. - Canon Flint.*"

This was very puzzling. I had no memory of my father coming to see me in the nursery at all. Had I blocked this completely? If this record was true, the visit must have taken place during my first few months at Father Hudson's, when I was still in the nursery, and probably I was still very confused. Or was it simply an invention on their part?

"My father came when I was nine," I said firmly. I remembered that visit very well.
She didn't reply.
"Here's a note from Canon Flint. He went to see your mother. He asks your father if your mother is over her depression. Your father says she is much better now. Your father was asked whether Karl was illegitimate? Yes, but he would have you at home. He says your mother's still not going to Mass."

She laughed, which seemed an odd response.
"He had a real heart; they weren't that enlightened in those days, your father did really want you."
"Oh, so she really was depressed then."

Then she read:
"Your mother writes to say that her husband would pick on her for the slightest thing. This is a note from Canon Flint. Then she writes to say that things are better now. John is working nights."
She looked at her watch and said "Oh, it's time for me to go."
"So, I will see you tomorrow then."
I didn't go home. I went to see some of the nuns.

Later on I went and spent the rest of the evening in the pub then walked around the Home and down the High Street until the morning when I had some breakfast with the nun from the kitchen.
I went to Miss Carroll's office again; she came in at nine thirty.
"You're late."
"Now *you're* telling *me* I'm late", she laughed.
She opened the records again.
"This is where you got to."
I started to read a letter from my mother sending the family allowance. Part of it was hand-written and the rest was written in shorthand and what looked like the scribble of a child.

There was also a note from Sister Catherine saying that she had sent Karl home because he had cut up a picture, the teacher had slapped his legs and Karl had stabbed her in the hand with a pair of scissors. *This had been reframed by Barbara Bellamy in a story including the phrase 'there was blood everywhere,' and her question 'do you have a desire to kill your mother with a knife?' So that's where she got it from.*

Then there was a school report; it read: "Karl is stubborn and does not take to discipline. He is becoming an increasing danger to both staff and children. He is maladjusted. Signed: Sister Catherine."

There was a note from a child psychiatrist: "Karl is of average intelligence and is a loveable child. He does not display symptoms associated with his background. I would recommend adoption for him. I have not read his records, but in my opinion he is not maladjusted."

In other words, he had disagreed flatly with Sister Catherine. How different my life would have been if Father Hudson's had listened to him? Why didn't they?

There were more letters from Sister Catherine and the psychiatrist. There were letters were written by me in red crayon to Canon Coyne from the Assessment Centre.

A letter from the child psychiatrist stated that Karl has an I.Q. of 90, and is dull. *In retrospect, dull seems an odd diagnosis. An IQ of 90 lies within the average range.* 'He is too old to board away at school.' *Crome Court and Besford Court were both boarding schools for children with special needs, so these must have been under consideration.* And then there was a note from the psychiatrist about starting at the Special School.

My mother wrote that she thought adoption would be best for me. There was also a note from Canon Coyne saying that "Karl is not a handsome child and that it may be difficult to find a family willing to adopt." *At that time he had become the administrator.*

But another note from Canon Coyne followed to say that he had heard from a civil servant in Somerset who was interested in adopting me. Then a note from my father's solicitors stating that adoption was out of the question. And suddenly a note from Canon Coyne saying that he thought I was legitimate. I breathed a sigh of relief; what a roller-coaster of emotions...

Later in a note Canon Coyne commented on my parents, saying, "I think this relationship is sick." My mother wrote to send the Family Allowance. The letter had a different Cardiff address on it. It said that she had the mumps and that she needed the money over Christmas. She asked how their Christmas had been and said she would make up the difference from the Family Allowance soon.
Canon Coyne replied to say that they had enjoyed a nice Christmas and that I was well.
'So she hadn't been lying,' I thought, *'in my first contact with her when she said that she'd moved'.*

Mr. Walker had written on my school report that I knew the difference between a prank and a practical joke but that I rushed into things without thinking.

There were notes on the divorce in 1974. A solicitor's letter enquired as to whether there was a Karl Bicknell in the Home. A letter in response informed them that Karl Bicknell was there and was fine. *'He was rejected from birth by his mother, his father keeps in contact with him, and he has just started at a Special School and is doing fine.'*

Another letter from my mother sending the Family Allowance said that John was out of work and asked if she could she make up the difference another time? There was also a note saying that my mother had rung and told them that although John might give the impression that he had a home for me he was just a smooth talker.

There were two notes by Father Tucker about Mrs Riddle and Mr Cartwright asking to take me out. Another letter from my mother, asking how much she owed, and a letter in reply from Father Hudson. A note from Sister Francis said that I wanted to be a painter and decorator and that I would like to be an impersonator like the ones on telly. I thought of my brother Paul; like me, so good at impersonations. Sister Francis, who used to beat me, had started to ask this kind of question after attending her residential social work course.

There were more letters from my mother about the Family Allowance. Her style of writing had changed; there were no more personal touches; she was simply conduction business transactions.

Mr Walker wrote on a school report that he felt I had a chip on my shoulder. And Mr Tissington wrote that I read books that were above my head.

My grandmother had completed a form for the Catholic Child Society, and there was a letter from her to Father Hudson's calling herself Mrs. Bitus, written when I was about 18. There was a letter from my step-grandfather Larry too, saying "please, please get in contact with Karl for his grandmother." Also my letter to Father Tucker asking him to forward a letter to my grandmother. It included a note saying "Don't work too hard," and a sketch of a letter with an arrow pointing to it.

A letter to me from Father Tucker said "Let me know how you get on." All he had ever told me was that my grandmother had rung the home to wish me a happy Christmas, before my mother ever made contact. I never knew that she and Larry had written several letters enquiring about me, when I was living at Plunkett House.

No contact was made with my grandmother until I got my flat; several **years** after she and Larry had written. *'Very clever,'* I thought, piecing it all together like this.

I found a note from Father Tucker to say that my mother rang saying how guilty she had felt about me, that Francine had known about me, and that my mother had had problems with having Francine, her first child. Another note from Father Tucker said he had given me a week to reflect on the proposed contact with my mother at St. Vincent's. He had written "Karl rang to say that he felt that he had known her all his life." I looked at this very hard and then put it to one side, thinking of the incident in the Priest's Dining Room where I'd said I felt I knew my mother all my life. He must have written this five years after the event and then put it in the file at the appropriate place; a form of forgery, or at least an element of deceit.

There was a note on a small piece of paper from Father Tucker saying that *'the adoption had gone well'*. This must have been about somebody completely different; he was a social worker dealing with fostering and adoption on a daily basis in the local mother and baby unit, but why it was on *my* file is a mystery. It also mentioned that *'some nutcase had rung that day asking if my father was really my father'*. This was also very cryptic in context. Presumably my mother had rung him and complained about me asking her whether I was legitimate or not. Next to this note was an enlarged photocopy of the same piece of paper. This seemed weird too; why had it been copied? Enlarging it meant that it could certainly not be overlooked.

There was a further note on the file saying that *'a relaxed Mr. Bicknell came to the Home today.'* This referred to the date of Gerard Rossiter's funeral. I thought about the rebirth therapy; I had been far from relaxed at that funeral, and they knew it.

I found one note from a social worker whom I had seen briefly when I came back to Father Hudson's. This was before Miss Carroll decided to take over the case, because of the issue of access to my records, which she refused. A note from her said *"Karl Bicknell walked into care looking a little lost today."* And another: *"Mr. Bicknell rang and said that he was suicidal. I was not very sympathetic, I thought he was drunk."* I remembered the conversation; she had told me to see a psychiatrist. At the time, I knew perfectly well that she did not want me to see a psychiatrist at all; not only was the whole Home in a state of panic because of Gerard's suicide, and because of other returning residents with psychological problems, but she knew perfectly well that she had already frightened me off psychiatry by telling me that about the woman who was not allowed to emigrate because she had had psychiatric treatment. These were mind-games; I knew it and they knew it.

There were two original reports dating from the time that I came into Care. I remembered Barbara Bellamy giving me two photocopies of these, years before. Those were the first records that I ever saw. One says 'Canon Flint received child from mother. Admitted to St Teresa's Nursery 16th November 1963.' The other is a Form of Application to Father Hudson's Homes made by John Bicknell my father on 16th November 1965. So maybe this lay at the root of the confusion? Maybe Father Tucker read the first (inaccurate) record and assumed this meant I was 18 months when admitted?

A note of the telephone call I'd made to Miss Carroll: "I was not disturbed *in* Care, I was disturbed *by your* care, and this is called reframing by telephone."

I looked at it. 'The clever bitch!' These were selective reception reports which gave no real background or feeling for an individual.

Just then Miss Carroll came in.
"How are you doing?"
"I think I've had enough."
"I can understand that."
She sat down.

"Do you do any therapy these days?"
"No."
"Do you think you have more control over your life now?"
"Yes."

"I met a man who had a very loving wife, but if he was under stress at work he would rock back and forth in bed."
"I just play with my hair."
"I do that too," she said, and pushed back her own hair. Was this true?
"And how do you relate to women?" she asked.
"I can distinguish between my mother and other women, that's not a problem for me. I don't want to know my parents now."

"Have you any political views, I don't suppose you do?"
"I quite like the Green Party because they're into the environment, and from a homeopathic point of view if you are polluted internally you will have a desire to pollute the external, and I am personally very much against therapeutic abuse."
"Yes, there's a lot of that around."
"Father Tucker pushed me into contacting my mother."
There was a slight pause.
"Yes," she admitted, "that was badly handled. You didn't have a very good youth," another pause, and then she changed the context completely, "what with your brother dying. What do you want to do with your life?"
"Do a degree."

She stood up and pushed the notes back to gather them up. "Oh, there's a note from Mrs. Bellamy about psychodrama," she said, and laughed. I didn't find this remotely amusing.
"And here's your mother's letter with the last Family Allowance payment. What's this? A school report: 'He is slow in getting in to his football kit.'" As if there was any significance in this.
"I hated football," I said, "that Special School offers you nothing. There wasn't even a carrot at the end of the stick."
"You should have gone to a Steiner school; you would have been more able to express yourself. I wish they would put notes back as they found them. Here's my own letter saying that Mr. Bicknell had rung to say that his mother

wanted to see him and that he had thrown a teapot though a skylight. He said that Father Tucker was trying to protect him, and I told him to write a nice letter to his landlord. Here's your nice letter, and here's my letter."
She touched a sheet of paper and put it back without allowing me to read it. These were completely separate incidents which she seemed to have consolidated, and I wondered why?

We left the room. As we were walking up the stairs I said
"Sometimes you slip up. I've got the original reply to the letter that I sent to your organisation. You said that 'as a private organisation we do not have to hand over the records to you.' Father Tucker rang me up at St. Vincents' to tell me my grandmother was sick, but it wasn't until years later that I remembered she'd rung and a contact was made with her. Father Tucker said he'd lost contact with my mother, when I asked about it during my mid-teens."

Chapter Nineteen

I came home thinking that Miss Carroll's letter of reply would be there, but it wasn't. So I rang Mr. Pinches.

"Hello", he said. "My wife thinks I should retire. What your records show is a picture of someone being consistently disturbed. That is not a full representation of the facts."
"Well, you write your side of the story"
I thought that would be impossible.

"Why did Mrs. Bellamy use a school report to suggest that I was in danger from my mother? And why did she say that I was referred to Care at eighteen months old when there is no record of that? If I'd committed suicide because of all this you would have justified it somehow, you would have swept it under the carpet. The only reason Mrs. Bellamy did that interview was because she was leaving; she would have no further responsibility for the case. Would you pass this message on to Miss Carroll. I'm just writing it down. Thank you."

Some days later I rang Miss Carroll:
"Did you get my message from Mr Pinches?"
"I've just got into the office."
I thought to myself *she's lying.* Just then I started to run out of money for the telephone.
"I'll have to ring you back."
"What's your telephone number?".

Some minutes later the 'phone rang.
"Hello."
"How do you feel now you've read the records?"
"Either my mother said that I was illegitimate in order to get me adopted ...."
"Yes ...."
"Or it was my mother being vindictive to get at my father for leaving when I was born."
"Yes ..."
"Or else it was true....?"

"Yes. Who would you say was the strongest of those?" "They're all as strong as each other."
"Your father really did care. He really did want you. Get in contact before it's too late to overcome his grief and yours. He really did suffer. I wish I could turn the clocks back for you."
"How?"
"Just tell him that you know different now."

After I'd hung up, and over the next few weeks, I felt so sad and confused. I wondered whether Mrs. Bellamy was telling lies about my father. I decided that because I had said that Father Tucker was trying to protect me from my parents Mrs. Bellamy must have been lying about my father. And then Miss Carroll had not confirmed two appointments, and on the telephone she'd said "four and a half" really quickly. When I asked about my grandmother she must have known what Mrs. Bellamy had said to me. She knew exactly what she was doing when she avoided answering the questions that I had given Mr. Pinches for her. She had asked me how I felt because I had asked Mr. Pinches how he felt. *'They just pass messages around to each other and give them back to you over the 'phone',* I thought. I remembered the interview that I had had with Mrs. Bellamy, she'd come across to give me a hug. I thought *'the filthy dirty pervert'* and tried to shake off the feeling remembering how she had sat there lying her face off to me.

"Your parents were playing you off against each other like a bat and ball."
"More likely you were playing me off against my parents like a bat and ball."
There was no note on file to suggest that a nun had gone to see my mother. And then they had said, "if ever we can help you we will."

I had spent years of my life in that Home, stuffed with surrogate aunts and uncles when I had the real thing in Cardiff. If they had given me some help I would have lived in Cardiff, and the family-feud would never have happened. And then they had lied in that interview with Mrs. Bellamy. They would not have wanted my grandmother to get in contact with me because it would have messed up things for them. Why hadn't she told me all those years ago to get in contact with my father? When I asked Miss Carroll for the records the first time all she did was to keep me dangling for a year on the 'phone, knowing that they weren't obliged to give me access to their records.

Every time I go and see these people it's like getting an electric shock. They give you all the right information in the wrong place and at the wrong time, and they know there's nothing that you can do about it. When you think you have resolved all your problems they pull another fast one. How could I get in contact with my father? She didn't even confirm the appointment. I had no proof that I had an appointment.

If I'd gone to see my father he would've been confused after I'd called him a spiteful vindictive bastard over the telephone. He was right, I decided; he'd said I knew fuck all. I suppose we will have to live with this for the rest of our lives. And his feelings had never changed from the time that he came up to see me. He would think I was mad after I had said that I'd read the records. How could I explain that was the first time I had seen the records?

I could understand why my mother had wanted me in Cardiff to please my father and have me integrated into the family. I understood now why she didn't tell the rest of the family; what was the point in telling them if I was in a Home in Birmingham? And maybe my father had stopped coming because of Coleshill's decision about Cardiff. They did not want any contact with the family. They were just trying to fuck my writing up too; all those notes I wrote before, they were a complete waste of time, I thought.

I decided I'd go round to the Post Office and send a recorded letter to Miss Carroll asking her for a copy of her letter allowing me to see my files. I thought that if I had some evidence that it was not until today that I had seen my records for the first time then I might be able to explain to my parents the reasons for my behaviour over the years, and how Coleshill had attempted to sever my relations with them. But Miss Carroll might not sign for it, and that would show them that I didn't believe that they had sent off the letter confirming the appointment with Miss Carroll. Even if I were to ring and ask them they would probably say that they had sent the letter confirming the appointment, but that it must have got lost in the post.

I just ran round the town with my head full of it all. It was the same game that they'd played with my mother. One of their nice mental loops that has you running around inside yourself, and they're not lifting a finger to help you unless it's on their terms. Then they write down that you came into Care looking lost, but they never say why. You ring them up feeling suicidal and they tell you to see a psychiatrist. They know you're worried about the possibility of going on a psychiatrist's file, and it messing up your life. Then they write something completely different on your records. They all walk around with "We Care About You" stickers on them, knowing you can't afford their therapies. But you have to depend on them. The only reason they paid Dr Willy is because it was cheaper than paying the compensation for the nervous shock that the contact with my mother had caused me due to their misinformation.

Not only were they controlling my life in Care but also my life outside as well. The last thing they want on their records is a letter from Willy saying there's some improvement. They achieve their goals by their client being disturbed all the time.

It reminded me of a book that I had read once about an experiment with a monkey. They had put two bricks with food on them in a cage; one was green and the other was red. Then they electrified the red brick and as the monkey put his hand out to get the food he got an electric shock. The monkey learned not to touch the red brick. They repeated the experiment with the green brick and the monkey displayed all the symptoms of having been rejected. He sat there acting withdrawn and confused and pulling his hair out; just like in a modern day crucible play.

I imagined kicking Miss Carroll's face in for what she'd said over the 'phone. It occurred to me that if I did that in real life I would go to court, which would be a great injustice to me. It would confirm their belief that people who have been abused go on to abuse others. I could imagine them saying "It's the social workers who are the real victims, look what we have to put up with." I would never give them that satisfaction.

I rang Mr. Pinches, the receptionist said that he was busy. "Would you tell Miss Carroll that I'm not responsible for what social workers say to me. Could she ring up my father and tell him what she said to me?"
"Who? Your father or your mother?"
"My father."

I thought *'she won't get in touch with my father because he will have realised that the Home has made slanderous statements about him to me behind his back.'*

I rang Miss Carroll some days later:
"Did you get in con tact with my father?"
"I think you misunderstood. How could we tell you that your mother was writing guilty letters? I told you to get in contact with your father in order to get over your loss."
I slammed the 'phone down then rang Mr Pinches.
"I've just spoken to Miss Carroll; she treats people like puppets."
"And what is she saying?"
"One minute she's saying get in contact with your father to help him get over his loss, and the next she's telling me to get in contact to get over *my* loss. And 'how could we tell you your mother was writing guilty letters .' She just treats people like puppets. Would you speak to her, I'm trying to keep the peace, I don't want to rake up the past. I suggest that you look at the records."
"I will, I understand that your situation is a very complex one."
"Thank you."
'That will have no effect at all. The only reason it's complex is because you make it that way; it's quite simple really,' I thought to myself. *'If they can say this in private about my father then they can say it in public.'*

I went to the solicitors and explained what had happened over the years.
"We must find out whether they have a 'duty of care", he said, and cracked a joke:
"Were there bars on the windows to stop you falling out?"
I couldn't stop laughing at the thought of what he'd said.

The solicitor's letter arrived some weeks later.

Dear Mr Bicknell,
Thank you for calling at the office on 17th and 28th May, following our meeting on 16th May. I have now prepared a draft letter to send to the Father Hudson's society as discussed, and perhaps you would like to check through the letter and let me have your views before the letter, either in this or an amended form, is sent.
Yours sincerely,

The Principal,
Father Hudson's Childrens Society,
Coleshill,
Warwickshire.
30 May 1991

Dear Sir or Madam,
Re Mr. Karl Anthony Bicknell

We have been consulted by Mr. Bicknell in relation to his childhood care by your Society, following his move to Canterbury. We understand that on the 29th April, Mr. Bicknell visited your Society and was allowed access to the records kept in relation to him, but that he is still unclear on a number of points concerning his childhood, as follows:-

When did Mr.Bicknell come into your society's care and in what circumstances?
Were both his parents involved in this placement?
Were Mr. Bicknells' parents married to each other?
When did Mr. Bicknells' grandmother first contact your Society and what response did you give?
What contact did you have with Mr. Bicknells' parents during the period he was in Care and was the question of adoption ever raised by either of them or with either of them?
Why were no steps taken to move Mr. Bicknell to Care in Cardiff following his mother's request that this should be done?
Was Mr. Bicknell's father informed of Mrs. Bicknell's request?
Why was our client not allowed to inspect your Society's records when he first requested to do so via his previous solicitors ?

We understand that at that stage our client was instead offered an interview with Mrs. Bellamy and that he was informed that a case conference was to take place before this meeting.
Do you have notes of the case conference in question ?
Do you have any notes of the interview which took place between our client and Father Tucker when our client was in his mid teens, asking about his parentage ?

Can you explain to our client why Miss Carroll was so concerned that he should contact his father straightaway when he spoke to her over the telephone after being allowed to see his records in April, and why did Miss Carroll say that she was sorry and wished she could turn the clock back ?

We look forward to hearing from you concerning all of the above points so that we can advise Mr. Bicknell further. We are grateful to you for your assistance.

I rang Miss Carroll.
"Take your time." It was like putting my head on speed when she said that.
"You know that I can't take my time, you did not confirm the appointment."
"I've just been to the solicitors to ask you about ten questions."
"Oh, what are they? I can answer you now."
"You will have to wait, there's lots of way to tell a child that he has been abused, like saying his mother was sick at the time."
Just then the money ran out.

Weeks later a letter arrived:

Father Hudson's Society July 1991
Father Hudson's Homes Coleshill Birmingham
Confidential.

Dear Sirs,
re: Karl Anthony Bicknell.

Thank you for your letter of the 10th June in which you request answers to ten questions posed by Mr. Bicknell. He asked similar questions of Miss Carroll when he came here on April 28th to read though his file.
Most of the questions would be better answered in a private counselling session and this is something we have consistently offered on a number of occasions over the years. You will appreciate, of course, that certain matters are confidential between the Society and those with whom we were dealing at the time. There may well be matters that we are not at liberty to divulge without the consent of the people concerned.
However I am able to give some factual answers to the questions posed but only in so far as they can be answers from our twenty-six year old file.

What counselling ?
Karl Anthony Bicknell was received in the care of Father Hudson's Homes on the 16th November 1965 at the age of three years and ten months at his mother's request.
It would appear that Mrs. Bicknell was the prime mover and that Mr. Bicknell acquiesced.
Yes.
A Mrs. Britos 'phoned in December 1978 and was advised to send Karl a letter or card to Coleshill and we would pass it on. (He had in fact transferred to St. Vincent's earlier in the year.)
Is that a fact.
Mrs. Bicknell wrote to the Homes occasionally during the early years but this seemed to cease in the September of 1969. It would appear that she again made contact by telephone in the February of 1979. The question of adoption was considered but, in the event, it was not possible to make a placement.

But she did send the Family Allowance with an address. They missed out the contact with my father too.

The whole question of the possibility of moving Karl to Cardiff was explored with the Cardiff Catholic Rescue Society and it was deemed in Karl's best interests to remain at Coleshill. When discussing this in April, Mr. Bicknell said he understood why this decision was made. I have no idea whether Mr. Bicknell's father was informed of Mrs. Bicknell's request.

Bellamy knew what to say about my father.

There is no correspondence from another firm of solicitors on the file but I have a vague recollection of a telephone call from a firm saying that they represented Mr. Bicknell. If I remember correctly they were talking about legal rights and I advised them to address themselves to the Society's solicitors, Messrs. Gateley & Waring. Mr. Bicknell has never been denied details about his origins.

That was a clever way to get out of that one.

I can find no record of a case conference being held but Mr. Bicknell did have an interview with Mrs. Bellamy who has since left the Society's employ.

Well of course there's no case conference on the file.

The notes of interviews between Mr. Bicknell and Father Tucker have been read by Mr. Bicknell.

There was no note of an interview in my mid teens.

If I had tried to prosecute them in the past Father Tucker would have said in court that he had given me a week to think about it contacting my mother, which would have meant that it was my fault.

On reading his file, Mr. Bicknell became aware that Mr. Bicknell Senior had actually cared about him, despite the fact that he had not actually prevented him coming into Care. Mr. Bicknell stated in April that he had always harboured bitter thoughts about his father as well as his mother. Miss Carroll suggested that Mr. Bicknell should bridge the gap with his father, given Mr. Bicknell had expressed greater understanding regarding the emotional condition of his mother in the circumstances. In saying that she "wished she could turn the clock back" she meant that because Mr. Bicknell had expressed bitterness about his lot in life, that she wished things had been better for him, ie. that he had been able to experience a conventional family life and a sense of belonging. These were not always possible for children placed in Care twenty five years ago.

What a nice switch from themselves to my parents. Playing their Erickson strategy and reinforcing their Freudian beliefs about your childhood problems; they never let you forget what happened twenty odd years ago, nothing, ever changes; they just move the goalposts for you.

Yours sincerely,
M. J. Pinches.   DIRECTOR.

Chapter Twenty

I rang Miss Carroll. I was in an uncontrollable fit of rage. I was shouting down the phone:
"I don't feel bitter about my mother and father, I feel bitter ..."
"Karl, Karl," she responded calmly; so calmly that she sounded really patronizing.
".... at the way you treated me, you knew exactly how I felt coming away from that interview. You great big mental loop bitch. Tucker claimed in the Priest's Dining Room that he knew nothing about the ...."

"... I'm glad you're getting it out of your system Karl; go and see your doctor."
"....abuse, and Bellamy was lying. If the Society knew that you had played off an abused child against ...."
"Go and see your doctor."
For me, this mention of doctors triggered the memory of being told that visiting a psychiatrist could ruin my chances of ever emigrating.

".... both his parents, they would be shocked. You clever, clever great big mental loop bitch on a 'phone." I slammed the 'phone down.

Some weeks later I rang Mr. Pinches.
"I had no idea that I'd had bitter feelings about both my parents all my life. Why was I unable to move down to Cardiff; because my brother and sister lived there?"
"Well, your mother wrote and then stopped, so she must have changed her mind. I think your father must have gone along with her."
"No she didn't. *You* changed her mind. You wrapped her up with bureaucratic red tape and told her to fuck off."
"Now now, how do you know, you weren't there."
I was thinking *'You wrapped me up with your bureaucratic bullshit about access to my records, so you must have done it to her, too.'* "If Father Tucker said that I was put into Care at eighteen months and Mrs. Bellamy said that I was referred to Care at eighteen months why is there no record of it now?"
"I don't know what's in the minds of my social workers."
"Thank you."
I put the 'phone down.

"You seem to know exactly what to say when it comes to covering yourselves," I said aloud to the air. I thought of what Miss Carroll had put on the records; that she had been unsympathetic to me on the phone when she thought I was drunk.....

I rang up again and spoke to receptionist.
"Can I speak to Miss Carroll ?"
"She's just gone out."
"Did you know that they had re-sequenced my Personal History for me on two occasions? It would be obvious to them that I would agree that Father Tucker was trying to protect me, after the brain washing they gave me, wouldn't it?"
"I don't understand all this. I only work here part-time."
"Would you pass a message onto Miss Carroll then, to say that she ought to remove the remark that she was 'unsympathetic when I said I was suicidal' from the file, as that would mean that I couldn't prove that they were unsympathetic to me either. Thank you."

Some months later I went back to Worcester to get some of my clothing from a friend's house. Looking through all my belongings I found the copy of the solicitor's letter that I had in fact sent off to them from Worcester. It was not the letter that I thought I had sent.

10th August 1988.

Dear Sir,
We act on behalf of Karl Anthony Mark Bicknell, date of birth 13th of January 1962. Mr. Bicknell spent his childhood in the care of your Society. He is now anxious to obtain access to the records surrounding his admission into Care.

We believe he has telephoned your Society in an attempt to obtain these records without success.

We enclose Mr. Bicknell's written authority for you to release these records to us, and should be grateful if in the circumstances you could release them as quickly as possible. We look forward to hearing from you with the records within the course of the next fourteen days.
Yours faithfully,

The Director,

Father Hudson's Homes, Coleshill,
Birmingham   c.c Mr. Bicknell

I came back home and made an appointment to see my solicitor. I showed him the letter.

"Yes, there's no doubt that they messed you about. The right hand doesn't seem to know what the left one is doing. As I said before, the only way you can prove this is to prove they damaged you mentally in some way. All this is because there was new legislation for interviewing in Children's Homes; abused children are messed up anyway. Well, I will write about it so long as it's true. That's what we've got freedom of the press for."
"Truth's all abstract to me; it depends on how well you cover your tracks."
"That's true."

I rang up Mr. Pinches.
"Did you pay Doctor William?"
"Yes, he has been paid in full."
"About Father Tucker's interview, since when has a single question been answered in the plural?" (*His notes had said 'I have seen notes of interviews' but I knew there had only ever been one interview, and when I had looked at my own records I found no notes even of that one.*) "I'm running out of money," I said, "will you ring me back please?" The 'phone went dead, and then rang again..

"Hello." It was Joyce Carroll this time. I felt confused.
"Don't you want to speak to me?" she asked, "Mr. Pinches is busy."
"You're such a fabulous liar," I responded
"Don't call me a liar, you're being very rude."
"Have you removed your remark that you were 'unsympathetic' from the file?"
"No."
"Remove it."
"No."
"Because there was no legislation governing those interviews it meant that you could lie after I'd contacted my mother. I had a breakdown which you never put on your records."
"I think you're having a breakdown now, go and see your doctor."

"I know why you said that. Are you trying to say that I can't distinguish between what is real and what is not real?" No reply.
"Mrs. Bellamy lied to me, and you never confirmed my appointment with you."
"It must have got lost in the post"
"How very convenient."
"I'm going to write down now that I regret letting you look at your records."
"You're getting a kick out of this," I said, desperately.
"You're wheezing on the 'phone, go and see your doctor."
I thought *'she'll use that to stop me looking at the files, I won't listen to her distractions.'*
"I know why you said 'you shouted at your mother, but you're shouting at *us* now'; you're getting a perverted kick out of this."
"I 'm writing it down. I wish I'd never let you look at the records."
"You're getting a great big kick out of this one you great big pervert, because there was no legislation governing those..." The phone went dead.

Chapter Twenty-one

Willie Monteiro suggested to me once that the best way to revenge yourself on a person is to do better than they do. I certainly didn't want any more psychotherapy, so I decided to write a history of what had happened to me. I began to draft this biographical fragment.

Presently I spoke again to Joyce Carroll. "You're very bitter about society," she said. Did she mean Father Hudson's Society, or society in general? I told her that I was writing the piece in order to improve the quality of my life. It seemed to me that it was up to the most articulate members of the community of care-leavers to make public what had previously been a very private issue.

When I had finished my first draft, which I wrote at the University of Kent in 1992, at the suggestion of a sympathetic lecturer in the Law Faculty I applied to various universities to read sociology or politics or both.

At that time the courts were almost flooded with cases of child abuse against Care homes, and my story was part of that zeitgeist. I got an unconditional offer from Middlesex to read sociology. I was thrilled.

I immediately applied for a grant from Kent LEA. To my surprise, Father Hudson's gave me £500 towards moving; there was money in trust for old boys.

On the strength of this, I moved to London and found some digs in Tottenham, next door to Smiley's Garage. It was all quite middle class; there was a desk and a Welsh dresser. After Whitstable, London was incredibly noisy and busy; a stark contrast.

But the LEA lost my grant application. If I couldn't pay the rent or the fees, the whole dream was over.

By now it was September and I was getting desperate. I felt that I needed to tell my parents that I thought Father Hudson's had treated our whole family badly. I rang my father to try to explain this, to tell him about my university place, and to ask him for a loan to tide me over. He didn't offer any congratulations, and refused absolutely to lend me any money, saying he and all other members of the family were 'skint'.

I spoke to Francine, who was living in London; but she rejected me too. I suggested we meet up. "I don't know what my plans are," she said.

Eventually my grant did come through and I survived.

I rang my mother up and told her that I had written this piece. "That was very vindictive of you!" she declared, and slammed the phone down. Conversations became more and more difficult and recriminatory. I tried to communicate to my family the confusions that had arisen about my going into care, interviews, lies etc. But my mother didn't want to know any of my experiences of Father Hudson's at all. She was still only angry at my presence at my grandmother's funeral, which had 'embarrassed' her.
Suddenly she told me that my brother Paul had died six months earlier. This was a bombshell; I was deeply shocked. He choked in his own vomit, she told me.

I went to visit them at Cardiff, and was made to feel totally unwelcome. My mother behaved like a prima donna; she said that Paul's death was effectively nothing to do with me, as I didn't really know him. "He wouldn't listen," she said, "he was just like Stefan in that way." She implied that both these deaths, Stefan's and Paul's, were of their own making. Ultimately I was shown the door.

Later I discovered from Aunt Elizabeth that my father was not skint at all. He had received his redundancy money in September, and they had remarried. So they really did not want to have anything to do with me, or to know anything about me whatever. Their instincts as parents seemed to be in reverse gear.

Soon after this conversation I spoke to Shaun. He took my mother's part, and reinforced what she had said, that I never really knew Paul. Whose fault was that, I wondered? Shaun went on to say that he couldn't have anything to do with me, because 'Mum would go up the wall.' This seemed contradictory; I was being blamed for not knowing one brother and prevented from knowing another.

Finally they went ex-directory, and I have never spoken to any of them again. Later I spoke to Joyce Carroll on the phone. I said that if Father Tucker hadn't lied to me by omission, by withholding vital information about my family, I would never have made contact with my parents. Moreover, the Society would never have received two separate solicitors' letters about my case.

"You didn't even know Father Tucker," she replied. "Do you feel the victim?"
"Yes," I replied, "I do."
"I was taken off the case because I found it all too stressful," she claimed, and put the phone down.

'So what do you think it's been like for me?' I asked myself.

Chapter Twenty-two

By 1998 serious cracks were beginning to appear in the care system, particularly the Catholic care system. I was in Canterbury nick at the time I read about cases that were being brought by former care residents against their former carers. One name leaped out; Eric Taylor was a priest at Father Hudson's Home in the 50s and 60s. Now he was exposed as a paedophile who had abused many boys in his care, and he was imprisoned for seven years in 1998. What really grabbed my attention was that a newspaper article in the Birmingham Post mentioned that 'detectives found hundreds of boys' files hidden away at the home, stuffed with letters and cards they were sent but never got'. I had never been abused sexually, but this was another kind of abuse; had the Home been hiding letters from my parents? Or from my grandmother?

At last I had the courage to pursue my problems again and rang up the Worcester Evening News. A reporter came to interview me, and an article by Simon Newton was published about my case in July. The article quoted the current director of Father Hudson's, Kevin Caffrey, as saying that 'there's nothing to hide. If Mr Bicknell...wanted to write to us we would be pleased to offer him the service we have today.'

In October the senior social worker at Father Hudson's told me they had located my records but that I was on a six-month waiting list for their release. Clearly they had been deluged with demands for records as a result of Eric Taylor's conviction. She also said that it would be helpful to have my mother's consent to my having copies of letters she had sent to the Society.

I went to a new solicitor, and explained what had happened to me. She wrote to my parents asking for permission to allow the release copies of their letters, and enclosing the article about me. As I half-expected, there was no response to this (clearly they were either embarrassed or simply wanted to forget the past).

But it was possible to get round this; the solicitor explained that we were talking about an action for negligence, could go to court and get a 'pre-action disclosure' which meant that if Father Hudson's did not consent to release my records it would demonstrate they had something to hide.

All in all, this was a very emotional time for me.

Finally they did release my records. In amongst them was a photocopy of a note apparently made by Father Tucker in February 1979 when I was 17. He recorded that Mrs Cathy Bicknell had rung him out of the blue and 'wondered about Karl.' 'She related' the note went on ' how she thoroughly rejected Karl years ago as she was unbalanced at the time' and 'deeply regretted having done so.' 'Saw doctor and various people but no help was so forthcoming. Background circumstances were that she went through a bad period after having 1st daughter. Husband only wanted a boy and she couldn't take it. She was half schizophrenic when boy arrived and rejected him. Felt awful relief when eventually she was parted with [sic] him. ... oldest girl vaguely aware of existence of Karl. Others not told. Story told to oldest was that mother was looking after someone for a time. Said she would welcome hearing from Karl and suggested Monday day or evening as best time if he wished to ring her.'

Father Tucker had added on March 5th: 'It was following Friday before I conveyed this to Karl and I suggested he reflect on it and ring me on Monday which he did. I then contacted his mother later and arranged fro Karl to phone her this evening at 7.30p.m.'

This was an amazing document and I couldn't stop reading it. If Father Tucker had told me all this about my mother, would I have contacted her at all? Certainly my thinking processes would have been very different. I might have left the whole situation alone for years. His failure to take responsibility for me or my mental health and well-being made me absolutely furious. I was only 17 at the time. Should I not have had some counseling to help me before trying to deal with this extraordinary situation?

Queries about this led to a declaration from Father Hudson's solicitors that 'they have no information as to whether there had been a system [of counselling] in place in the late 1970s,' and that 'such information is not available on record or elsewhere'.

Presently the Worcester Evening News published an article about my case. I wanted to write a fuller account of my life and publish it, but I was worried that it might be libellous.

I consulted a new solicitor, who thought I might have a case against Father Hudson's, and she asked a barrister for an opinion.

Counsel's opinion was that any case I might have against the Society would be based on negligence, but such a claim only allows a three year period, and the time began when I became 18 in 1980. So time ran out in 1983, and it was now 2000. Although the court has some 'residual powers' to extend the time limit, that depends on circumstances. Counsel thought that as I had been in a position to take proceedings earlier, I would not stand much chance in bringing a civil claim. In this case, he went on, the establishment of negligence needs a three-fold test; 'establishing a duty of care, setting up the standard of that duty and proving a breach, and thirdly, showing causation'. Although he thought I had an arguable case, he thought I would have great difficulty in establishing, for litigation purposes, that there was negligence. 'A more definitive answer would need to come from an experienced sociologist with knowledge of standards of thirty years ago'. So overall, he was saying that the public expense of full investigation could not be justified.

He also said that if I was looking for compensation, I would need to show that my psychological damage was the result of acts of negligence by the society, and that 'causation might be difficult to establish'. So overall, his advice was that my prospects for establishing civil liability were less than 50%, although the genuineness of my case was not in doubt.

So there was no prospect of compensation. My best hope was for an apology of some kind. In 2001 I contacted Archbishop Vincent Nichols, a very sincere compassionate priest, now Archbishop of Westminster. I talked to him at some length. He had never heard of Father Tucker, but he agreed with me that the role of social worker and the role of priest were incompatible. He was sympathetic and concerned, and asked what kind of help I needed? Did I ever go to church? he asked. No, I said, I have not set foot in a church since for years. He seemed a bit concerned as to whether I would really publish a book about my life and experiences.

Scripts

Eric Berne wrote about the way 'scripts' may govern our lives.
Some of us may live out the script for the eldest child, or for the youngest, or for the invalid, or for the tear-away; all quite unwittingly. Until we become aware of the script written for us, we cannot break free of it, as it is buried in our unconscious mind. When we do become conscious of it, if we dislike it, we can rip it up and start again.

Usually these scripts are written by the family in very early childhood, before we are consciously aware of them. What sort of script is written by an institution?

What script was written for me by my family? And did Father Hudson's simply take that script over, lock stock and barrel, or did they try to write a new one?

My first script was written by my mother. According to this, I was at fault, marked out as trouble, as impossible to deal with, as too much for her to accept. She wrote for me a script whereby I would be adopted by another family, and everything in the garden would be rosy. But this script didn't work out. My possessive father realised that it was him or me; if I stayed she would leave him ('I'd have him home in Cardiff but the wife would divorce me'). So he went along with my going into care. But he couldn't accept the second chapter of the script; he would not allow me to be adopted. His script for probably me being accepted back into the family ('I was hoping things would work out'). This was mental cruelty. So I was caught between two scripts, and landed in Father Hudson's for fourteen years.

What script did the institution write? To some extent, it simply wrote a continuation of the same programme ('Karl has one or two problems which make it impossible for him to be fostered'). But it wrote another one too; a Catholic script by which every child in care would leave that care knowing the love of God, living within the family of the Church, in the habit of prayer, with a strong moral framework within which to live and work, and devotion to the sacraments (baptism, marriage, and the mass). According to this script, I was a child of God, and a boy to be educated in such a way that I could earn a living and go on to marry and settle down with a family in continuation of these values.

But their efforts to educate me were to a large extent foiled by my dyslexia. Although Father Tucker did call in Mrs Riddle to try to help me, at that time in the '70s very few people had even heard of dyslexia, let alone trained in how to teach the dyslexic child. Many dyslexic children feel a deep sense of frustration and fury that, while other members of the class are not so intelligent, nonetheless they can do this one magic trick of reading and writing which earns them kudos and good marks and approval. This rage often persists into adulthood; the percentage of dyslexic people in prison is far higher than the norm.

So in a way they continued the script that said I was impossible to deal with, and impossible to educate. I had to go to a special school; I was a failure. In fact, in educational terms, the Father Hudson's script failed. I could only get a dead-end job.

At this moment, when I was seventeen, the scripts clashed. My father was still clinging to an old script that said one day my mother would allow me to be accepted back into the family; and this script was so strong that I had internalised it for myself. My mother was still clinging to an old script that said I would grow up to be happy and that when I was an adult we would accept each other. By this time the Father Hudson's script was patently coming to pieces, so Father Tucker tried to adopt my mother's ('two or three meetings will trigger off an acceptance').

This clash of scripts occurred when my mother made contact with Father Hudson's, and my subsequent contact with her was handled with a radical lack of preparation and support. So I fell between two scripts once more, feeling some sense of loyalty to my family, some sense of loyalty to Father Hudson's, hopelessly confused and rejected all over again. The religious script written for me by the Catholic church fell apart under the shock; particularly when I lost confidence in the priest who had taught it to me. My mother's script fell apart under the shock too, as I realised that she could not accept me back into the family, ever. So I was left without a script.

Anybody can go through traumatic experiences and survive, but this usually needs careful therapeutic work. If a traumatic experience is expected, such as the re-introduction of a child to his parents after fourteen years, careful sympathetic preparation is clearly necessary. Nowadays such preparation is hopefully the norm; policies are in place; staff are trained. Follow-up procedures, counselling, support, advice are hopefully on offer. But for me, these support systems were not in place. And nobody was prepared to take responsibility for what happened to me. So I had to try to find therapy for myself.

The barrister who ultimately advised me suggested that I was effectively suffering from post-traumatic stress disorder. So I am not surprised that my life has been difficult. PTSD is notoriously difficult to deal with. I have received psycho-analysis, Transactional Analysis therapy, and alcohol counselling in my time. The most helpful techniques seem to be NLP techniques such as I was taught by Dr Willie Monteiro and promulgated by e.g. Paul McKenna. From my perspective, talking about my life and my problems didn't change anything; it just made me very tired and reinforced my distressing memories. 'If you keep on rehearsing a script, you get to learn it by heart'. I also found homeopathy helpful, and acupuncture; neither of these demand endless talk about one's life. What works for one person doesn't necessarily work for another, but I pass my own experience on for what it's worth.

I must also put my own experience as a care leaver in perspective.

Research broadcast by the BBC in 2008 showed that at that time 12% of children in care got five good GCSEs compared to 60% of all children (I got none).

Only 6% of care leavers in England went on to university (I was one).

A quarter of those in prisons were at some point in care (I was one).

A third of those living on the streets had been through the care system (I was one).

At a conference run by Dr Jim Goddard in London in all these points were highlighted, together with many others such as mental health problems (I had them), alcohol problems (I had them), and so on. Work is continuing on this front.

But the writing of this account has helped me to feel that perhaps my life has not been a total waste of time. I hope other people with similar histories will find their own way to a light at the end of their tunnel.

Printed in Great Britain
by Amazon.co.uk, Ltd.,
Marston Gate.